# So You Think You Are

# Ready To Retire?

The Retirement Lifestyle Center

ISBN: 978-0-692-23348-1

# Acknowledgements

## Barry LaValley

This book has been in the works for several years. While I have delivered over two-hundred workshops over the past decade on retirement, I have been unable to "find my voice" when it came to putting my ideas into a book form. There was so much information and the challenge was to get the content into a form that was easy for the reader and included the most important points that I wanted to make.

I want to thank some people who encouraged me along the way to share the information that is contained within. To my friends Gavin Murray, Amy D'Aprix, Heather Compton, Myles Morin, Mark Finke and Rhonda Latreille, I appreciate the ongoing nudges to make this a reality for me.

To my friends Jeff Steele, Dave Inkster, Rod White and Jan Jarvie, I value the input you gave me on the text.

To my graphic designer Laura Timmermans and my researcher Vesna Crnkovik, thank you for the hard work you did!

To my editors, Rosemary McCracken and Ed Piwowarczyk, I appreciated the depth that you went to uncover and correct my grammar and punctuation.

To Gillian Leithman, Janet Segerin-Lopes, Av Lieberman, Andrew Roblin, Lee Anne Davies and Mitch Anthony, thank you for your influence on me and my ideas over the years.

Finally, to my wife Melissa and son Peter, I appreciate your ongoing love and support for what I do. I dedicate this book to you.

## Mark Finke

Barry LaValley put his life's work into these pages for all of us to enjoy and learn from. As a result, I am thrilled for myself and anyone else that picks up this book. I will never be able to thank him enough for the honor of collaborating with him. Barry's wit, his deep insight into what really makes for a successful retirement, and his ability to convey all of this information in a fun and informative manner makes it easy to want to listen to him and learn from him.

In addition, Barry's passion and heartfelt desire that every person might have the knowledge necessary to enjoy a fulfilling and happy retirement has helped me and many other advisors put clarity around what our real role is in the lives of our clients.

In addition to my gratitude to Barry, I owe special thanks and appreciation to many people in my life, most notably:

Tom Mengel, Chuck Surdyke and Tom Murphy, my friends and business partners for two decades. Together, we have put Barry's strategies for a "happy retirement" in place within our firm and have seen wonderful results with our clients. Over the years, Tom, Tom and Chuck, as well as the teams at MSMF Wealth Management and Sonus Benefits, have allowed me the privilege of working alongside them each and every day serving our clients.

Dan Sullivan, Mary Miller, and Stephanie Song from Strategic Coach© for teaching me to dream, that there is "more", and then figuring out how to actually make it happen.

Kim DeMotte, our "Corporate CoDriver" at MSMF and Sonus, for teaching (and re-teaching!) me that being in my "Natural Child" is a great space to be in.

Brandon Dempsey, Derek Weber, Bronwyn Ritchie, and entire team at goBRANDgo! for their energy, expertise and support (and patience) through this process.

My parents, Walt and Rosemarie Finke, for all of the life lessons they taught me, especially that "good enough" isn't really either one of those things.

My "Princesses," Rosie and Gracie, for giving me the best job anyone could ever ask for and reminding me, when I see their smiles, why God put me on this Earth.

# Table of Contents

## Part Six: Enjoying Your Lifestyle

## Part Seven: Your Money And Your Life

## Part Eight: Your Second Life Plan

# *Foreward* by Mark Finke

Ron walked into my office. He had been retired for four years and wasn't happy with the advice he was receiving from an advisor in our area. We sorted out his portfolio, talked about his needs and concerns. He related a story to me that caused me to reexamine how I was addressing retirement with my own clients.

"Mark, when I retired I thought that my life was going to be easy. I had money and I had a vague idea of some of the wonderful things that I could do now that I had all of this free time. Haven't I worked hard for a long time? Don't I finally deserve a permanent vacation?

On my first day, I slept in until 10 o'clock. My wife had already gone to work and I was left alone with my thoughts. Funny, but my first thought was not that I was excited—instead, I questioned myself for being 'lazy'.

Throughout the day I reflected on my life. Was it really over now that I was retired? Would I still be "relevant" and feel like I had some value? It never occurred to me that I might feel this way—after all, retirement was supposed to be a bed of roses and here I was already questioning it on my very first day.

If I had to do it all over again, I would have spent more time on the transition rather than focusing on the destination. I should have spoken to more people who had gone through the same thing. They could have shared some of their experiences and helped me understand the 'secret' that no one tells you about.

Retirement is a big life transition. It shakes you to your core and causes you to reexamine everything about your life, your relationships, your health and how you view the world.

Nobody tells you about the stress. I smiled when I thought of my former financial advisor who had less of an idea about retirement than I did. Talk about the "blind leading the blind"—he figured that all I needed to do was to get the money right and everything would fall into place!

It has taken me the past four years to stop spinning my wheels. In a sense, I have wasted precious time adjusting to the realities of retirement. For example, you can't play golf seven days a week because it becomes a chore rather than an enjoyment.

Today my wife and I recognize that retirement doesn't automatically mean happiness and that we haven't become 'new' people. I'll tell you though, we are a lot smarter now."

It is for clients like Ron that I chose to seek answers to questions like his and broaden my own understanding on all of the issues that come with retirement. It has enabled me to provide my clients with a more balanced perspective on this next phase of life.

Mark Finke
St. Louis MO
May 2014

# Introduction

## PREPARING YOUR MIND FOR RETIREMENT

When you think of your retirement, what vision comes to mind? Will this be a life of leisure after work with no responsibilities? Do you think of it as the beginning of a 30-year-long weekend? Have you drawn up your bucket list yet?

For most North Americans, retirement planning is a financial exercise. If you have done the "right" things, contributed to your IRA or 401K plan over the years and received good advice on managing your nest egg, you can say that you are ready for retirement. In fact, one financial services company in the U.S. starts its commercial with the question, "Do you know your number?"

Apparently this means that if you have accumulated that number prior to retirement, then you are well on the way to enjoying a wonderful life after work. Once your financial situation has been settled, you can sit back and enjoy the rewards that retirement brings.

### Are You Ready For Retirement?

If we were also to ask the question, "Are you ready for retirement?" and you were not allowed to consider your financial issues at all, what would your answer be? Do you feel that you have the right attitudes, personality and outlook to get the most out of this next phase of life?

It is far too easy to think of retirement as if it were the same as an extended vacation and not to consider important issues that will help you get more out of your new circumstances. Many participants in our retirement workshops come prepared to sit through two full days of financial exercises and information on pensions, income strategies and investment advice. They are quite surprised by the extent of the life issues that they understand intuitively but had never considered important in their retirement plans.

Retirement planning is more about assessing how you live your life today and how you want to live it in the future. One of the biggest misconceptions about retirement is that it is the beginning of a new life and that you become a "new" person.

Retirement is a continuation of your present life. You are who you are and always have been, but now is your opportunity to live the kind of life that you truly want. You could put yourself through this exercise at any stage of life, but your move into retirement is a very good time to sit back and assess how you think and feel about this life that you are living now and into the future.

Some might call this "life planning," but we prefer to think of it as "life awareness" that gets you back in touch with who you really are. If you can understand yourself, you will be far more able to develop retirement goals and plans that go beyond a bucket list or the purchase of a winter home with palm trees.

## Working with my retiring clients

In my wealth management practice, I try to help my clients understand the real problems we are dealing with and discuss solutions in language that they can understand. I then can coach and empower them to use their resources in a manner that enables them to live their "second life" filled with purpose.

We don't simply pull a "blue" or "green" transition strategy off the shelf for our clients. We educate and coach our clients through the process of designing an integrated plan that reflects the life they want to live, not one I think they should.

I have spent several decades questioning the supposed "wisdom" surrounding retirement planning. While I have a degree in engineering and a mind for data, I also realize that we live our lives far beyond the numbers. I have never been comfortable with how the financial services industry prepared people for retirement by focusing solely on the money. The reality is there are dozens of studies that have shown money is only one of several priorities in preparing for a transition into a second life. This "great failure" of our industry left me dismayed and looking for answers on just how to effectively coach clients through this process.

I first came across Barry LaValley's work and research several years ago when a colleague shared one of his presentations with me. That "eureka" moment started a mentorship, collaboration and friendship that helped me answer that burning question regarding the missing ingredients to a successful retirement transition. And I am thrilled to say it also resulted in this coaching guide that will set you on the path of living a second life filled with purpose!

Barry LaValley is the President of The Retirement Lifestyle Center and has delivered hundreds of retirement workshops throughout the United States and Canada to thousands of pre-retirees. Barry employs a similar coaching and teaching style that I use that focuses on allowing individuals, couples, and partners to develop their plan, not someone else's.

The material that follows is the result of Barry's twenty-five years of work in the field of retirement, psychology and transition issues faced by pre-retirees around the world. He has combined his understanding of retirees and what they go through with the research that is available in the social sciences.

Most retirement books tell you how to retire. They claim that you should do this or you should do that. The problem with that approach is that we are all different—not everyone is an extrovert or a self-starter. Some of us just don't like other people, which makes it hard to be advised that we need people in retirement.

This book has been designed to help you work through your own thought process as you consider your retirement transition. Throughout the book, we will share with you the most recent research on various life issues that you should think about or at least be aware of. In addition, we have put together some thought-provoking exercises that will give you the opportunity to get your own thoughts and ideas together.

## Changing The Way You Feel About This Next Phase Of Life

One of our goals is to consider retirement from the standpoint of how people feel about their lives. As such, we want to take advantage of the tremendous body of research that exists around the world to consider the psychology of retirement. What makes this approach different? It doesn't start with financial or workplace issues but from an emotional perspective.

We make no assumptions about your marital status, age, financial situation and desire to retire. We also understand that not everyone sees a glass half-full or is a self-starter just looking for a blueprint for the perfect retirement. Your retirement is just that—your retirement. However, we can provide you with some things to think about that you may not have known or understood that will help you get even more out of this next journey.

*Our research suggests that:*

• Self-starters tend to do better than "other-directed" people and that most of us have the ability to become more self-directed persons.

• Optimists tend to do better than pessimists, but then optimists expect to do better than pessimists! We are all different and yet sometimes a new way of looking at something like retirement can change our level of optimism.

• We tend to do better in our lives (and certainly in retirement) if we have nurturing and supporting relationships. However, there are many who don't like to spend time with other people and prefer their own company to friends and family.

• We gain more life enjoyment when we look after both our mental and physical health. We all know this, but perhaps we haven't understood the power of healthy aging on everything from our personal happiness to our longevity.

• We need some of the things in retirement that work once provided us. It is far better to take some of the positives from work and bring them into retirement, but there will always be people who think that everything about work was evil and that prolonged leisure is the main benefit of retired life.

All of these things we can prove scientifically. Whether you want to incorporate them into your life will depend on your own personality and your willingness to change. The self-starters and optimists will not have major problems making adjustments to their outlook—after all, they have been doing that all their lives and that is likely what has made them who they are.

Others are not used to making changes in their lives and are entrenched in their thinking. Our view is that this book has to serve everyone and that we are not telling you to be anyone other than who you are. All we can do is give you some things to think about.

## But What If I Am Not Outgoing, An Optimist Or A Self-Starter?

Don't panic! We're not consigning your retirement to a state of unhappiness just because you don't like people, are not outgoing or are not internally driven to make your life what you want.

It takes all kinds of people to make a world and our retirement model respects that there are going to be differences. We look at the overall picture as a bell curve. Since retirement is all about how you frame things, are there opportunities in your life to frame them in a different way? Can you see the positives more than the negatives?

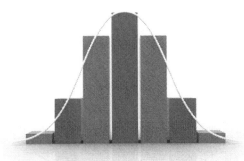

Where do you fit on the curve? If you are closer to one side, continuity theory (see Chapter 8) says that you may find it more difficult to change; self-awareness is not as effective in moving you away from your predispositions. However, if you are somewhere in the middle, there is an opportunity for you to change how you frame the world and how you feel about your ability to make changes.

Mindset can be changed, partly through self-awareness and partly through believing that you can change the way that you look at things.

*Here are some ways that you can change your mindset for retirement:*

**1** **Get the best information you can.**
Talk to as many people as possible who have something of value to offer you on retirement education. (And thank you for reading this book, by the way!) This could include psychologists, financial advisors, career specialists, doctors—in fact, anyone who has expertise in the areas we discuss in this book.

**2** **Model yourself on other successful people who have a skill that you would like.**
This could include friends who seem to have the ability to make things happen or others who may be good at making friends. You also want to look at other successful retirees to see what they are doing and how they look at their retirement.

**3** **Look at your beliefs and decide if they will limit you in retirement or not.**

In this book we offer you some thoughts on what the best practices might be for retirees based on how they see the world. We also give you plenty of opportunities to examine your beliefs, and how you frame your life and your attitudes.

**4** **Shape your visions of this next phase of life!**
Decide on the goals that you want to achieve and then list the positives and negatives that come from the way that you view the world. Change your limiting beliefs by creating a goal and a plan to achieve the goal.

**5** **Believe in yourself.**
Hear you own voice (to quote noted motivator Stephen Covey). It is easy to listen to everyone else and then make a decision on what you want to do. Trust yourself. Take in wisdom from elsewhere but be discerning about the input you get. You have control!

## How To Use This Book

This is meant to be a coaching guide that you can use as a catalyst to build your own plan and create your own mindset for retirement. The format is based on two simple questions:

1. **Did you know?**

2. **Have you thought about…?**

The "**Did you know?**" sections address key issues in each area of your retirement life. We have used five areas as the template to look at your life and apply your thinking and goal setting:

**1** **Your work:** Not only leaving it, but also incorporating it into your Second Life;

**2** **Your approach to healthy aging:** Looking at both the mental and physical aspects of getting older;

**3** **Your relationships:** Nurturing and supporting the relationships that will be most important to you in the future;

**4** **Your lifestyle and leisure:** Living each day to the fullest and finding retirement happiness;

**5** **Your sense of "financial comfort":** Using your financial resources effectively to ensure that you achieve everything that you want in your Second Life.

Each chapter focuses on one element of the overall life area and we have grouped the life areas together. We have also included some exercises within each area that have been designed to help you think about the subject at hand. These are meant to be to be used as "food for thought" and a great way for you to organize your thoughts around each area.

## The Only Retirement Book That Matters

We want you to think about what your own retirement is going to look like and how you feel about that. Many people assume that their retirement will unfold like everyone else's. Too often, they are really clear about what they are retiring *from* but not entirely clear about what they are retiring *too*.

This "new" retirement will require a different approach to planning as well as a much broader frame of reference for retirement advisors and coaches. Retirement planning for today's North American boomers will be viewed more as a transition than a destination.

You have the opportunity to build the kind of life you want, and accomplish some of the things you dreamt of when you thought you'd have all the time in the world. While we now know our time is not without limit, we have the experience that we can apply to make each of our moments count.

Someone once said, "There are many books available on retirement, but the only book that *really* matters is the one that you write for yourself!"

Rather than writing another book on retirement, we wanted to provide you with a new way of thinking about your transition into this next phase of life.

# PART 1

*THE CHANGING NATURE OF*
*TODAY'S RETIREMENT*

# CHAPTER 1
## Not Your Parents' Retirement

### SOME THINGS TO CONSIDER:
• What does the word retirement mean to you?

• Will your retirement look like your parents' or grandparents'?

• Do you want to retire or is it just something you assumed you would do?

*The purpose of this chapter is to open your mind to what retirement is and what it is not.* Our goal is to encourage you to define retirement in your own terms and not based on what the adverts say. Generally, people take a romantic view of retirement and don't consider it a continuation of their present life. We want to establish that retirement is a transition rather than a destination!

I was due to meet with my client, Allison, to go over her retirement portfolio and talk about the effects of volatile markets on her plan. I liked working with Allison. She was a 57-year-old dynamo who seemed to have 20 different projects going at any one time. She never seemed to be too worried about the vagaries of the markets and continued to put her money into equities regardless of what was happening on Wall Street. "There is no sense calling this my retirement account," she would say. "Since I am never going to retire, why don't we just refer to it as my long-term savings plan?"

I started to think about the word retirement and what it actually meant to someone like Allison, who clearly had no intention of quitting or retiring in the traditional sense. We had her money in a "retirement" account, and we talked about retirement as if it were a mandatory rite of passage, one that she was choosing to ignore even though we tend to think of anyone over 65 as a "retiree."

## Redefining Retirement

*When you wake up one morning and decide that, from this day forward, you can do what you want, when you want and how you want, you are retired.*

—Barry LaValley

There is an old story that can be used to describe how many aging boomers think about retirement. A woman who was preparing a dinner for her family cut the end off of the roast before putting it into the pot. The daughter asked why she did this and her mom said: "I don't know. That is how Granny always did it. Go ask Granny in the living room why she did it that way." Granny's response was that the pot she used was too small for a roast and that was why she always cut the end off of the roast. So some 40 years later, the practice continued unquestioned, even though the woman now had access to bigger pots.

If you were to ask the average person on the street to define retirement, he or she might say that retirement means that his or her work career is done and that they are moving to a life of leisure. Others might relate retirement to their financial situation and their ability to do whatever they want.

We look at retirement in the same way that the mother learned how to cook a roast. She simply took the approach that her own mother had taken without considering why. 'Retirement' means what it always has-- the holiday at the end of a work career.

Throughout North American social history, there are few moments where an entire generation has made such a paradigmatic shift in lifestyle and outlook. As the first wave of baby boomers pass their sixty-fifth birthdays, they are faced with a collision of forces that will affect virtually every aspect of their lives. Concern about health issues, the changing nature of the workplace, family dynamics, issues with parents and children, and financial worries will be the catalysts of change.

As a result, baby boomers are about to reinvent retirement. They have to because the traditional view of retirement they inherited from previous generations no longer fits who they are. But it wasn't until they were on the verge of retirement that they began to realize that their concerns, opportunities and needs necessitated their own approach to this next phase of life.

## 'Retirement' Is Becoming Irrelevant

In fact, the concept of retirement that we have accepted for these many years will likely disappear from common usage in the next generation or 25 years as increasing numbers of boomers make the transition. This doesn't mean that retirement itself will disappear: it just won't mean what it used to for earlier generations.

The words 'retirement' and 'retired' no longer refer to whether one is working or not. Instead, retirement has become synonymous with choice and freedom rather than with leisure and old age.

The retirement assumptions based on society's views of work, health and "getting older" will all be challenged. In the past, retirement was a rite of passage that came automatically at the end of a work career. This period of life was called 'Third Age" to emphasize that it was part of a new life.

The Third Age model suggests that our first age was one of education; our second focused on our work careers; and our third was one of leisure.

The Third Age concept no longer fits today's model, which encourages us to include elements of education, work and leisure at all stages of our lives. Many Americans will continue to work into their 60s, 70s and beyond; they will do so not because they need the money, but because they have stopped demonizing the word 'work' and consider it to be an important break from leisure.

## Your Second Life—It's In Your Mind!

The Japanese have an interesting concept to describe this phase of life. They call it Second Life and it refers more to a state of mind rather than a workplace or financial issue. The Japanese believe that when a person reaches middle age, he or she becomes a "respected elder" in society. The respected elder has gained a perspective on life that comes from introspection, experience and perspective.

The interesting thing about the Japanese concept is that it relates more to who you are rather than what you are going to do. It is an internal concept. Entering Second Life means transitioning one's mind into this next stage of life.

This is the period in your life when your family responsibilities have changed and you can focus on your "inner peace." It is a time when you get closer to your soul and dispense your wisdom to benefit younger generations.

## This Next Phase Of Your Life Gives You The Opportunity To:

• **Find life's meaning rather than "resting."**  This next phase of life gives   people the opportunity to tie their life plan more closely to the values and life goals that they may have had but didn't have the time for when they were working.

• **Achieve life balance over lopsided leisure.** While retirement for some is one long-weekend, your retirement can be a fulfilling combination of quality leisure, satisfying work and a pursuit of self-knowledge.

• **Realize lifelong dreams over time-filling fun.** Setting goals can be a fun way for retirees to let their minds create wishes and then let their heads create the strategies to turn wishes into plans.

# CHAPTER 2

## The Realities Of Today's Boomer Retirement

### SOME THINGS TO CONSIDER:

• Is your vision of retirement really yours or your parents'?

• When you think of retirement, what vision comes to mind?

• Is retirement a destination or a transition to something else?

The perception of retirement and related challenges is distinctly different for the boomer generation from the experience of their parents' generation. A recent survey by Harris Interactive found that "retirees increasingly no longer regard retirement as an extended vacation or time of rest and relaxation, but rather as a new, active stage of life." Let's look at some of the challenges in this chapter.

**1** **Retirement is a Multi-Phased Journey**
Most retiring baby boomers can expect to be "in retirement" for at least 25 or 30 years. Retirement is no longer one long phase of life, but many distinct phases. The fact is that retirement is no longer a goal in itself or even a single destination, but a journey and a transition into the rest of your life.

**2** **Lack of Long-Term Financial Resources**
Many Americans lack the financial resources to finance their dreams of "30 years of fun," and are postponing planning for retirement in the wake of stock market reversals, job changes, increasing tuition costs, etc. A common refrain that financial advisors hear from clients is, "I may have to phase in my retirement because I don't think that we can afford it yet." And some people who have retired are realizing that, in fact, they can no longer afford to be "retired."

Market volatility has instilled some apprehension in people. For aging boomers, it has shaken them into realizing just how unprepared they are for retirement. Losses in their retirement nest eggs have caused a lot of people to rethink their visions.

Too many boomers are entering their 50s and 60s with mortgages, and high debt loads. This trend has been observed over the past decade as increasing numbers move toward their retirement date. Today, the ratio of U.S. household debt to income is one of the highest in the industrialized world.

When American real estate prices soared in the early part of the last decade, boomers used their increase in equity to add to their debt rather than to pay it down. The soon-to-be retirees appeared to be more concerned about lifestyle than about long-term security.

## 3 Supporting Children and Parents
Many of today's pre-retirees face the problem of having children still at home while dealing with aging parents who also require support. The concept of the "sandwich generation" has become the "club sandwich generation" for some households. In some cases, there are adult children living at home and boomers providing caregiving for older parents at the same time.

According to a Pew reseach study of U.S. Census data in 2013, over 36% of boomer households still have adult children living at home. Couple households with children account for about 60% of boomer households. About 55% of boomer households have children under age 18 and 36% under age 12. In addition, 12% of boomer households have a parent living with them and 23% currently provide monetary support for parents.

Many have underestimated the cost of sending their children to university, recalling a time when annual education and living costs were $500 per year compared to $30,000 to $50,000 annually today. With 55% of boomer households with children under 18, this expense may be a more pressing concern than saving for retirement.

## 4 Changing Work Environment
The workplace has changed over the past decade and this will have a significant impact on how retirement is viewed. Not only do we have more women in the workplace, but also there is a significant move toward self-employment, working at an older age and part-time work.

On the financial front, the declining availability of defined benefit pension plans has undermined many Americans' financial health.

## Not Your Parents' Retirement

Finally, today's baby boomers enter their 50s and 60s with a different view of the world than previous generations. This is perhaps the most influential reason why the retirement picture will undergo such a paradigmatic shift as the boomers seek to redefine it.

Boomer demands on the world they live in may force a variety of shifts in our culture. Consider these possibilities:

• **Ill Health:** Concern about the onset of chronic disease and the desire to do whatever possible to postpone physical aging will put additional pressure on the health-care system and will likely be a catalyst in changing the way services are provided.

• **Vitality:** Boomers are thinking and feeling younger and healthier—changing even further our perception of "elderly" and "retired." U.S. author Gail Sheehy suggests that boomers have added 10 to 15 years to the spread between their chronological and physical ages when compared to their parents. At 50, according to Sheehy, boomers are the same relative age as their parents were at 40.

• **Wealth:** Earnings, inheritances and return on investments provide some boomers with increasing amounts of discretionary dollars. Analysts such as Harry Dent have drawn the relationship between the need for boomers to save for their retirement and the non-stop bull market that dominated the 1980s and 1990s. In the future, many boomers will be able to start their own businesses and create the kind of lives that they aspire to.

• **Poverty:** Not all boomers are in a financial position to finance all aspects of their "self-actualization," and there will be an increasing disparity between boomers who can afford the kind of lifestyle that they want and those who can't. Many will have to continue working just to have a basic lifestyle and forgo a lot of things that make retirement special.

• **Demands on Social Services:** As they become empty nesters, caregivers, grandparents, widows and widowers, and eventually require specialized care themselves, boomers will put pressure on the overloaded social support system to expand services and change the dynamics of family relationships.

• **Spiritual Awakenings:** The psychological shift from the pursuit of material possessions to the pursuit of enjoyable experiences that nurture internal needs will likely foster a new "spirituality" or a search for clarity in values in order to gain more fulfillment. This could have a positive impact on the boomers' contributions to society.

• **Fun Times and Family:** A change in the way we define leisure, and the need to get more out of leisure activities in order to keep them special. This should lead to an absence of "disposable time" as our lifestyles become more complex and time management takes on even greater importance.

• **Impact of grandchildren:** If you have grandchildren, how does your interaction with them make you feel? Many people relocate, and alter their leisure-time goals and schedules to increase their contact with their grandchildren. While not everyone feels the same, a lot of boomers view their grandchildren as a life reaffirming gift and consider them a vital part of any retirement plan.

## The 10 Biggest Misconceptions Around Retirement

**1** **Retirement is a destination rather than a transition.** Many Americans are clear about what they are retiring from, but not clear about what they are retiring to. They often feel that retirement is this new life phase that is an extended holiday or a 30-year-long weekend.

**2** **Retirement could be the longest single phase of your life.** People believe retirement is a new life, the Third Age. In fact, you will go through six to eight distinct phases in your retirement, driven by either your health or the health of those you care about (spouse or partner).

It is a multi-phase journey. Also, remember that time isn't always your friend—getting older means doing as much as you can as quickly as you can. (Never put anything off!)

**3** **Retirement happiness is directly tied to how much money you have.** In fact, good health is probably the biggest key to a successful retirement. Happiness in retirement is a function of having a positive outlook, engagement in life, nurturing relationships, life meaning and a sense of accomplishment.

**4** **Retirement spending will be the same throughout retirement** People tend to spend like drunken sailors in the first few years of retirement before settling into a pattern. As time goes forward, spending tends to move more to family and health. Travel patterns tend to move toward less stressful travel and almost no travel in later years.

**5** **Three hundred rounds of golf a year are always a good thing (if you like to golf).** In retirement, as in all phases of life, too much of a good thing is often too much of a good thing. Golf because you want to, not becuae you have nothing else to do..

**6** **A life full of leisure must also be a good thing.** We like our holidays and weekends when we are working, so imagine if that were now our lives. Consider the paradox of leisure: we like leisure because it is a break from work. If we had leisure seven days a week for 30 years, where is the break?

**7** **Retirement is a 'couples' issue.** In fact, it is more likely to be a single woman's issue. The average age that a woman first becomes a widow in the U.S. (if she is going to be a widow) is 56. Sixty per cent of American women over age 65 are single, widowed or divorced according to U.S. Census data.

**8** **The goal of financial planning for retirement is to "reach your number."** There are issues that you will have to deal with during retirement such as income, tax and estate. Financial planning doesn't stop at retirement. Just because you have financial security doesn't guarantee retirement success. You still have relationship problems, health issues, happiness and sadness.

**9** **You can put things off in retirement.** In fact, you want to do as much as you can as quickly as you can. You never put anything off in retirement. Do it now and hope that you can do it for 30-plus years!

**10** Retirement is a time to do new things. It is, but as we age we actually have increased difficulty doing new things. Remember that you are who you are and that generally if you didn't do something before retirement, you will be less likely to do it after retirement. Since the retired "you" is no different than the working "you," ask yourself whether you are comfortable doing new things now. If not, you will have to create the positive strategies to do new things rather than assuming that time is the only variable.

## DID YOU KNOW?

• According to Swiss psychiatrist Carl Jung, our life is divided into two phases. During the first phase of life ("morning"), we focus on the external world of developing the ego. During the second phase ("afternoon"), we shift to developing the inner world of our true selves.

• According to Stanford University, two in three pre-retiree men underestimate the life expectancy of the average 65-year-old man. Of that group, 42% underestimate average life expectancy by five years or more. Roughly half of pre-retiree females underestimate the life expectancy of the average 65-year-old woman."

• A Léger Marketing survey conducted for the Bank of Montreal (BMO) in 2012 showed that 47% of respondents had discussed their ideal retirement lifestyle, 46% had talked about what age they want to retire at, 44% had mulled over where to live, 42% had talked finance and just 36% had discussed whether to sell their homes.

*"What will I do when I retire? When I quit my job, I don't want to quit living. Can I possibly be of use when my retirement day comes, or will I just be taking up space?"*

— Client at workshop

# CHAPTER 3
## Visualizing The Next Phase Of Your Life

## SOME THINGS TO CONSIDER:

• What do you want the next stage of your life to feel like?

• What changes do you anticipate?

• What are you most excited about and what do you fear most?

• What are the key values that you want to guide this next phase?

*The purpose of this chapter is to help you clarify where you are now in your thinking and focus you on your views of retirement today.* What does it mean to you? How clear is this picture that you have in your mind? Remember the old saying, "If you don't know where you are going, then how will you know when you get there?" The chapter will help you "clarify the vision" and subsequent chapters will either reconfirm your vision or get you to consider a change!

*"We thought that our retirement would unfold in the same way that our working life did. We would not have to think about anything, things would just happen and our life would go on as if we were on permanent vacation. After five years of retirement, we have taken the trips that we wanted and pretty much exhausted our love of not having to be anywhere. We still feel that we can build a quality life for ourselves and now we are talking about what that means and what we want to accomplish."*

— **John and Anna**, *retirees*

Okay, you are contemplating your retirement. You have probably developed some type of financial plan, including identifying whatever benefits you might be eligible for from your work. You are at the age where you have been told that you should start to think about retirement; in fact, someone may have suggested that if you can stop working when you are younger, you can consider yourself to be a great success!

Assume for a moment that your vision of retirement is to stop working and have 30 or more years of leisure activity ahead of you. Round-the-world trip? No problem, as long as you can afford it. After all, you have all of the time you need to do whatever you want. Right?

At a recent workshop, a woman shared her plans for her retirement. It was clear that she was financially comfortable, although I sensed that she might have thought that she had far more money for retirement than she actually did.

"I want to do a lot of travelling in my retirement," she told me. "Every year, as often as I can, and to every place that I have always wanted to go."

When I asked her how much time in an average year she'd take to go on her trips, she said she thought "at least three or four months each year."

"And for the other eight months?" I asked. "Have you thought about what you are going to do when you are not travelling?"

"Hmm," she replied. "I hadn't really thought beyond my dream of travelling."

## When You Think Of Your Retirement, What Vision Comes To Mind?

Aaron and Monica Sector were approaching the point where Aaron could walk away from his company with a reasonable pension. Monica, an elementary school teacher, still had five years left before she joined her husband 'in retirement. The Sectors had been caught up in the task of raising a family, juggling careers and trying to "stay ahead."

Our discussions often turned to retirement planning and how Aaron and Monica were on track financially to 'never have to work again. They thought that if they could just free up their time, they could spend as much time as possible pursuing the things that made them happy. "I can hardly wait until I can wake up and know that I don't have to get to class," Monica told me one day.

I asked her what she would do instead. "Well, we certainly are going to spend more time hiking, and I have always wanted to focus on my garden." What do you think that a week of your retirement will actually look like 10 years from now? I asked. "I am not really sure," she replied, "but we will have plenty of time to figure that out when I quit teaching!"

It struck me that the Sectors "retirement plan" was based on being able to pursue activities that they like to do today. They hadn't considered how they were going to feel about their new life and what was really important to them. In thinking about my clients, I realized that many of them had similar views of the future: a fuzzy picture, an idea that they would all have all the time in the world to figure it out and a belief that having the necessary time to pursue hobbies and leisure activities was the only thing missing from having a perfect retirement life.

*Let's define your retirement in clearer terms:*

1 What does "being retired" mean to you?
2. What would an average week in retirement look like five years from now?
3. What challenges do you see along the way?
4. What fears do you have about this next phase of life?
5. What would you like to accomplish for yourself?

*People waste more time waiting for someone else to take control of their lives than they do in any other pursuit.*

— **Gloria Steinem**, *U.S. feminist, activist and editor*

## "He was worried he would have nothing to do when he retired."

## The Importance Of Attitude

One of my clients was not looking forward to her retirement at all. For the two years leading up to the day she would leave her job as a teacher, she fretted about what she would do and how she would feel when she didn't have to teach anymore. "It's funny, but I don't really even like teaching," she told me. "It's just that I have always been a teacher and when I retire, I guess that I will just be an ex-teacher!"

Often at our workshops, we talk to attendees who say they would love to enjoy retirement, but believe they don't have anything to look forward to. For example, a spouse may have passed away, or their financial situation may have some challenges, or they may feel bored with their lives.

The reality is that true zest for life comes from within and can best be nurtured by looking closely at your attitudes and view of life in order to discover the parts that may require some change and intentional rethinking! (Or fresh perspectives or conscious reframing or…) It is not what happens to you in life that determines if you are happy or content; it is how you feel about what happens to you and how you frame it. This is good news when you realize that you can't always control what happens to you, but you can always control your thoughts about your circumstances!

## What Gets You Out Of Bed Each Morning?

If you are going to make a commitment to live each day to its fullest, you will want to define what that means. *Here are some points to consider:*

• Why do you want to get out of bed in the morning?

• If you've made the commitment to challenge yourself to do new things or to learn new things, what kinds of challenges will make you feel good about who you are?

• What gives meaning and purpose to your life? When you assess and claim your values and sense of purpose for the future, you move toward happiness—and seize the opportunity to leave a meaningful personal legacy.

• The key is aligning your personal purpose, vision, and values with the activities and goals you choose to act on. With this alignment, your achievements will bring you real happiness—quite a different feeling from working to satisfy someone else's value system.

## The Importance Of Your Values

Your Second Life is a time for you to live the life that is true to the values that you have. Maslow called this state "self-actualization." Simply put, it gives you the opportunity to become the person you really are, free of the pushes and pulls of daily life. That is not to say that you are immune from demands or obligations, but that you have framed your life goals in terms of those deeply held values that define you.

Psychiatrist Abraham Maslow developed his 'needs' "needs" pyramid as a way to describe how our needs frame our actions. Some have interpreted the pyramid as a progression through our lives. However, a better way to look at it is to understand that we you may have setbacks along the way that will refocus us you on lower levels of the pyramid.

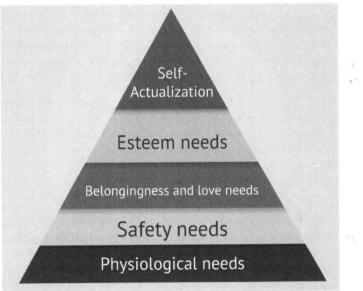

For example, a financial setback may drive you all the way back to your safety needs and your preoccupation to protect what you have. Similarly, earlier in life you may have moved to the self-actualization need and had everything below looked after. Suddenly, you lose a spouse and are left with a feeling of loneliness that focuses your attention on your need for social contact.

The lowest level of the needs pyramid that is threatened will be likely be your current concern. And that's the problem with getting older—there will be many things in your life that will move you up and down Maslow's pyramid.

The top two layers of the values pyramid represent your need for a sense of achievement—a driving force in your work life, but also in your overall life, including retirement. These don't go away, though many retirees feel that retiring from work also means retiring from the need to strive for something.

Values represent your deepest desires, including how you want to relate to others, to your world, to your sense of purpose. In fact, it can be argued that values are the key driver to your sense of personal accomplishment.

When you retire, that doesn't go away. In fact, if you have decided that your Second Life is going to be one of self-actualization, these will be the drivers of many of the important retirement achievements and goals that you have!

## What Are The Values That Will Guide Your Second Life?

Scientists have had a very hard time predicting a person's happiness, based on the good or bad events he or she has experienced. Instead, a far better predictor of happiness is the beliefs and attitudes he or she maintains. Our happiness is inextricably bound to the things in life that we value. Too often, however, we base our dreams of our future on activities or events that we would like to have happen without really understanding the real reason why those dreams would make us happy.

What is it that makes you happy? It stands to reason that if you could find a way to be happy each and every day for the rest of your life, you will lead a truly fulfilling life. We all strive to be happy but I am not convinced that we all really know what is at the root of our happiness. Have you decided what it is for you?

Remember the Peggy Lee song from the late 1960s, "Is That All There Is?" when she laments the fact that the reality of our lives sometimes doesn't live up to our expectations?

> *Is that all there is? Is that all there is?*
> *If that's all there is, my friends, then let's keep dancing*
> *Let's break out the booze and have a ball*
> *If that's all there is*

It's not the events that make us happy, or simply participating in the activities. It's how they make us feel, the emotions they create inside us. And our emotions are stirred the most when we engage in activities that are directly linked to our core values.

*Happiness is a function of our expectations, a principle that we will keep coming back to in this book. If your idea of happiness is to be able to play golf ever day in retirement and you find you can no longer golf, you can adjust your expectations accordingly and still be happy.*

Planning the next phase of your life has to move from activity planning and financial planning to a higher level. You must find a way to tie your activities, your money and your life to your core values. As you think about your core values, what will be the guiding lights that will drive your next phase of life?

## Creating Your Legacy

One of the hardest things for a speaker to do is deliver a eulogy. In the past year, I have delivered eulogies for two close friends who died far too soon. As I prepared my tributes to my friends, I was struck by the realization that all of the money they had or the things that they did or the places that they went really weren't going to form the basis of my remarks. I wanted to focus on who these fine men were as people, how they touched those they loved and who loved them, and what we will all remember about them.

As I plan the rest of my life, one of the opportunities open to me is to create the kind of legacy that I want to leave. While I have no control over the date of my passing, I can help shape the remarks of some future eulogist today. While I never care about what people are saying about me when I am alive, I must confess that I do care about what they say about me when I am gone!

For many of us, almost one third of our lives are still in front of us. Planning for our Second Life gives us the opportunity to be the person that we truly want to be.

## What's Really Important for Your Second Life?

We can get so caught up in the demands and details of our day-to-day lives that we lose sight of the true treasures of life. We are often reminded by a sudden shot of happiness when we hear a piece of music that reminds us of another time, or when we stop to contemplate the beauty of a sunset, or when we break out in a smile watching our children or our pets play happily in the yard.

Many of the things that we know are truly precious in our lives we learned when we were children, before our attention was taken away by the daily grind of making a living. This can be a valuable consideration as we contemplate our potential role as wise mentors to the young, instilling lifelong memories and shaping their values for the future.

- What are life's treasures for you?
- What life lessons do you want to pass on?
- Is it important to you to play a role in the lives of others?
- Will your life goals involve mentorship?

We will talk about the keys to retirement success throughout this book. Let us say at the outset that an underlying theme is the need to feel that we are in control of our lives. We can't always control your health, for example, but we can always control our attitudes toward health.

You can't predict life transitions or how the stock market will move, but you can always put plans in place to handle those eventualities that might affect your life. Thinking ahead and taking personal responsibility for your life is the foundation of a successful and satisfying retirement plan.

## How Much Do You Understand About This Phase Of Life?

There are many views of the ideal retirement picture, and most of us have some pre-conceived notions about 'retirees'. Here are 15 statements that have been made about retirement and represent some common perceptions of this phase of life. Do you feel that they are TRUE or FALSE?

_____1. "The key to a successful retirement is having enough money to enjoy your life."

_____2. "Retirement comes at a time when you can no longer contribute to the workforce."

_____3. "More than half of American retirees report being lonely, depressed and/or sad."

_____4. "There are very few employment opportunities for those people over 60."

_____5. "You should plan to live on 75% of your last year's income in your first year of retirement."

_____6. "The longer that you stay in the workplace, the higher your risk of dying earlier than expected."

_____ 7. "Retirement could be the longest single phase of your life".

_____ 8. "One of the best ways to enjoy retirement is to find replacements for those things that you enjoyed about work."

_____ 9. "Retirement is less stressful on marital relationships than when you are working full-time."

_____ 10. "Men experience a more difficult transition into retirement than women."

_____ 11. "Over one third of retired Americans report not having enough money to live the life that they envisaged in retirement!"

_____ 12. "If you don't continue to exercise your mind, you risk falling victim to cognitive decline or a shortened lifespan."

_____ 13. "To have a comfortable retirement at age 55, you need over a million dollars in the bank."

_____ 14. "There is a direct relationship as we get older between high stress levels and declining physical health."

_____ 15. "Only a quarter of Americans over age 65 are limited in their mobility by chronic conditions."

*See answers on Page 267*

## Let's Take A Quick Inventory Of Your Retirement Vision Today

In what year do you believe that your present work situation will change? *Choose the terms that will best describe this next phase:*

- ☐ Not working at anything
- ☐ Working part-time at the same job
- ☐ Working part-time at a new job
- ☐ Starting a new career
- ☐ Developing a second business
- ☐ Becoming self-employed
- ☐ Consulting in my area of expertise
- ☐ Perpetual leisure/relaxation
- ☐ Building or renewing social relationships
- ☐ Spending more time with family, friends
- ☐ Buying a new business

- ☐ Continuing to work full-time by choice
- ☐ Doing what I want, when I want
- ☐ Focusing on hobbies
- ☐ Travelling more than three months a year
- ☐ Education or study
- ☐ Learn new skills
- ☐ Volunteering or community involvement
- ☐ Developing talents
- ☐ Moving to a new location
- ☐ Addressing health or fitness issues
- ☐ Becoming more "spiritual"
- ☐ Managing my investments
- ☐ Doing what I do now

### At this time, the idea of retirement makes me feel:

| 1 | 2 | 3 | 4 | 5 | 6 | 7 | 8 | 9 |
|---|---|---|---|---|---|---|---|---|
| Sad | | | Neither Good nor Bad | | | | | Excited |

### As of this moment in my life, my retirement planning program could be described as:

- ☐ Well thought-out
- ☐ Just a financial plan
- ☐ Have had some thoughts about it
- ☐ Haven't thought about it
- ☐ Don't intend to retire

### What are your greatest concerns about the future?

- ☐ Not having enough assets or income
- ☐ Inflation
- ☐ Lengthy illness
- ☐ Difficult family relationships
- ☐ Moving to a new area and then not liking it
- ☐ Moving to a new home and then not liking it
- ☐ Being bored
- ☐ Not being productive or useful
- ☐ Missing my friends from my work-life
- ☐ Investment crisis
- ☐ Other _____

## When I Retire...

Complete the following sentences as many times as you can—when you think you have run out of ideas, wait at least two minutes and then see if more ideas come.

| *When I Retire*, **I Will...** | *When I Retire*, **I Will Feel...** | *When I Retire*, **I Want To...** |
|---|---|---|
| | | |

## Paint the Picture

One way to begin to control the future is to create a vision of what you want the future to look like. Below is a creative exercise to help spark possibilities and begin the process. **Let your vision be big!**

*Imagine you are flying a helicopter over your life in retirement. Write down everything you see that's going well regarding this time in your life. **Imagine!** See yourself as the person you want to be. Write as many details as possible. What are your feelings? What is happening? Don't edit anything and don't think too hard! Just write and keep the pen moving for at least three minutes.*

When we asked participants in our workshops what they discovered from doing this activity, they told us, "It allowed me to dream…it opened up possibilities I hadn't ever thought about before…I gained a clearer picture of the nature and quality of the life I seek for myself in my Second Life…I got a sense of excitement from writing about how I want to feel in my Second Life and I discovered that what I really want is to be active and involved in many different areas of life."

## Exercise

### Identify Your Values

Attitudes represent how you feel about things today; your values are your core principles that guide your life. This exercise looks at your values because you will tend to carry these through all stages of your life.

These values are fundamental to your outlook, your motivation and your life planning. Some typical values that people hold are listed below. Check off which values are important to you in your life today. If there are others that are important to you but aren't listed, write these in the blank spaces.

| | | |
|---|---|---|
| Adventure | Community | Security |
| Family | Truth | Trust |
| Knowledge | Honour | Compassion |
| Honesty | Kindness | Devotion |
| Comfort | Safety | Wonder |
| Friendship | Respect | Parenthood |
| Love | Freedom | Tolerance |
| Health | Relationships | Justice |
| Dignity | Humility | Exploration |
| Independence | Inner Peace | Achievement |
| Optimism | Success | Positive Emotion |
| Service | Joy | Engagement in Life |
| Power | Charity | Life Meaning |
| Spirituality | Creativity | Meaningful Relationships |
| Sharing | Faith | |

Take the five values that you feel will be the most important to you in your Second Life and note them in the column below. Do you know deep down what these five values really mean to you? In a brief sentence, write down what each value will mean in the way you live your life.

For example, if you choose *health* as a value that guides your retirement you might say that *health means living a healthy life by maintaining both my mental and physical health to the best of my ability.* You want to be as specific as you can so that you can solidify in your own mind what each value means to you.

***Decide how important each value is to you and rank them in order of importance.***

| Life Value | What does this mean to you in the next phase of your life? | Rank |
|---|---|---|
| | | |
| | | |
| | | |
| | | |
| | | |

*We will revisit your values when we focus on your leisure activities (Chapter 22) and your bucket list (Chapter 26).*

# Exercise

## The Importance Of Attitude

Let's complete a short assessment to help give you a snapshot of how you view this change in your life. Below you will see two sets of statements. For each of these statements, we would like you to decide which one is more representative of how you feel. Between each pair is a set of numbers from 5 to 1, which represent the strength of your agreement with one of the statements. If you circle 1 or a 5 it means that you *strongly agree* with the statement on either end. If you circle 2 or 4, it means that you *agree somewhat* with the statement on either end. If you circle 3, it means that you *neither agree nor disagree* with either statement.

| | | |
|---|---|---|
| I expect my retirement to be a very exciting period in my life. | 5  4  3  2  1 | When I look at the previous stages of my life, I think retirement will be very restful. |
| I'm looking forward to a lot of great opportunities after retirement. | 5  4  3  2  1 | Retirement is the end of opportunity. |
| I expect to call my own shots and be active and involved in lots of things. | 5  4  3  2  1 | Everyone else will be telling me how to live. |
| Changes are openings to possibilities. | 5  4  3  2  1 | I wish things didn't have to change. |
| Life can be funny. I'm going to look for the humour in whatever I do. | 5  4  3  2  1 | There is nothing funny about retirement. What good am I? |
| Retired people have a lot of advantages over younger people. | 5  4  3  2  1 | Retired people are mostly disadvantaged in our society. |
| This is going to give me time to make new friends of all ages. | 5  4  3  2  1 | My friends are all at work, dying or moving away. This is only going to get lonelier. |

| | | |
|---|:---:|---|
| Retirement is a great time to try some new ideas and to take some risks. | 5  4  3  2  1 | Retirement is no time to be taking chances. |
| Retirement is a great time to try some new ideas and to take some risks. | 5  4  3  2  1 | Retirement is no time to be taking chances. |
| I'm in a position to be creative and make some contributions to society. | 5  4  3  2  1 | I'm all used up. There's nothing left to give. |
| Maybe I can't run a four-minute mile, but I can still have a good physical life. | 5  4  3  2  1 | I'm broken down and getting worse. Why fight it? |

## What Might This Tell You About Your Attitude?

If your total is 40-50, your attitudes will likely lead you toward a happy, rewarding next phase of your life. If your total is 30-39, you are somewhat sceptical, but are open to possibilities of contented retirement living. If your total is under 30, you will need to develop more positive attitudes and approaches to the retirement phase of your life.

If you found that this exercise hinted that your attitude toward retirement life is not as positive as you might like, you might consider these questions:

• Are you happy with all parts of your life, or can you make some important changes in a particular area that would have a positive effect overall? *(Chapter 11 can assist you in making a plan.)*

• What things in your life do you really value? What things make you feel the most fulfilled? *(You might want to pay particular attention to Chapter 8.)*

• How much time do you spend on solitary relaxation, where you get a chance to meditate and contemplate the beauty around you? *(We have also addressed the importance of this in Chapter 8.)*

# Exercise

## Your Legacy

Consider the questions below to prompt ideas about how you'd like to create your own legacy:

*At your 80th birthday party, when your friends gather to honour you, what would you like them to say about you in these areas?*

- ☐ As a spouse/partner
- ☐ As a parent
- ☐ As a friend
- ☐ As a community-minded individual
- ☐ As an intellect

If you knew that you only had five productive years left to live, how would that change how you live your life today?

- ☐ It wouldn't change how I live my life today.
- ☐ I would spend less time working and more time doing the things I like.
- ☐ I would quit my job and spend the next five years having fun.
- ☐ I would spend the next five years trying to create my legacy.
- ☐ I would try to get the most out of the time I have left.
- ☐ I would focus more on family and relationships with family members.

## What Will You Do With This Information?

1. Do you feel that you have a realistic view of your retirement?

2. What areas of your life do you have to address to complete your picture of retirement?

3. Will the pursuit of these values lead to your Second Life happiness?

## DID YOU KNOW?

• The current life expectancy in the U.S. is 76 years for men and 81 years for women —a two- and three-year increase respectively since 1994.

• A Sun Life survey conducted in 2013 has found that, on average, Americans now expect they will be able to retire by age 66.

• Eighty-eight per cent of boomers say they will work past their eligibility for retirement. According to the AARP early retirement peaked in 1994, with only 22% of people over 55 working. Now that rate is 34%. Within 10 years, as many as one in four workers will be 55 or over.

# CHAPTER 4

## *How Prepared Are You for Retirement?*

### SOME THINGS TO CONSIDER:

• Now that you have a vision about this next phase of life, do you actually have the plan in place to achieve it?

• What (if any) changes should you make to make sure that your transition goes as smoothly as possible?

• Are there some misconceptions that you held that might have affected how you look at this next phase of your life?

*The purpose of this chapter to provide you with a baseline on how you feel about your retirement now and how you would define it.* As you go through this book, you may change some of your ideas about what you want to do and how you think about your future. Finally, we want to show you what successful retirees think and do.

## "I wasn't prepared for his retirement - less money and more of him."

## Planning For Longevity

As you think about your retirement plans, you'll also want to consider just how long you may have to plan for. Traditionally, planning for retirement was based on leaving work at age 65 and then holidaying for 10 years until you became "old" at 75. Perhaps this is where the concept of retirement as a leisure activity came from.

Today, longevity has changed how we think about planning. Consider the following from Social Security Administration in 2013

|  | Women | Men | Both will still be alive | One of you will still be alive |
|---|---|---|---|---|
| Survive to age 80 | 80.5% | 63.68% | 50.9% | 92.75% |
| Survive to age 90 | 44.2% | 23.41% | 10.42% | 57.51% |
| Survive to age 100 | 8.82% | 2.43% | 0.22% | 11.08% |

When we speak with couples at our workshops, we find that most do not appreciate that the surviving spouse may live for a long time after the death of the first spouse. While longevity statistics usually refer to lifespan from birth, if either you or your spouse (or both) are alive at 65 and in reasonable health, you can expect to live into your late 80s.

## How Would You Describe The State Of Your Planning Today?

OK, you are thinking about retiring (however you define that) and you know that you need a plan. Your financial planner has probably spoken to you about how a retirement plan is the same as a financial plan, and that you should focus on income planning, tax planning, investment strategies and an estate plan. You see commercials on TV that tell you that you need more than $2 million if you want to retire properly.

You could be forgiven, therefore, for thinking that you are prepared for retirement if you feel prepared financially.

However, this book focuses on how prepared you are *mentally* to move into your retirement. As we noted in the introduction, we are focusing on several areas of your life and your attitude that will have a major influence on how successful or "happy" your retirement will be.

These are the four most common retirement mindsets that we see in our work. Let's look at each one and we would like you to think about where you might fit. Remember that regardless of your particular mindset today, you can make some changes in outlook or preparedness to improve your comfort level.

| Comfortable and Concerned | Uncomfortable and Concerned | Unprepared and Confident | Prepared and Confident |
|---|---|---|---|
| Have a written plan | May have a written plan | No written plan | Have a plan |
| Think "I am OK" | Didn't save enough | Didn't save enough | Actively involved in planning |
| Depend on a financial advisor | Carrying debt | Not worried | Understand financial planning |
| Worried about future financial security | Cutting back on lifestyle | Accepted current lifestyle | Enjoy investing |
| Bothered by uncertainty | Worried about future | Ready to adjust to reality | Optimistic about comfortable retirement |
| Not sure you understand all of the issues | Tend to be pessimistic | Optimistic—will find a way to make this work | Continuing to access information |

## Comfortable and Concerned:

Often we see attendees at our workshops that have done some of the right things as far as their financial plans go, but still feel uneasy about their future. It's the uncertainty that bothers them the most, the things that might happen that they didn't expect. If you feel that you are in this category, take a close look at the major issues that will affect your retirement and strengthen your understanding. Then look at your planning and gain some comfort that you have considered planning in all of the areas that you have control over.

## Uncomfortable and Concerned:

This is the category where pre-retirees need the most help. Not only do they feel that they don't have enough, but they are also concerned about their future. There is always some positive planning that can be done. If you are in this situation, the first step is to outline the areas of your life that will require a plan. Then, take an inventory of the resources that you have available. If there is a gap, then you should work with an advisor to find ways to close the gap.

## Unprepared and Confident:

These individuals haven't made a plan, probably don't have enough for the life that they dream of but somehow figure that it will all work out well! It is a good thing that optimists live longer than pessimists, though not if you don't have a plan. If you are in this situation, a written plan is a good start.

**Comfortable and Confident:**

On the surface, it appears that these individuals still require the least help. However, you still need support in your ongoing planning. There may be some things that either you didn't know or didn't consider which may help you be even more confident.

## What Can You Learn From Others?

While today's boomer retirement is a lot different than that of previous generations, you can learn a lot from other people who are already retired. Generally, people who are successful in their working lives will carry that success into their next stage of life.

## Exercise

### Learning From Others Who Have Already Retired

Think of someone you know who has retired. They could be current or past family members, friends, acquaintances, co-workers, etc. Picture what their days look like: How do they handle their retirement? Do you think that they are generally happy or generally unhappy?

*Here are a few questions that may help you envision their retirement.*

• What factors have made their retirement successful?

• What could have improved their retirement lives?

• What personal characteristics have added to their retirement success?

• What personal characteristics have detracted from their success in retirement?

# The changes that I wish to make in my planning are:

| Here are the changes I wish to make to my current planning | Here are the specific steps that I am going to take to incorporate these |
| --- | --- |
|  |  |

# PART 2

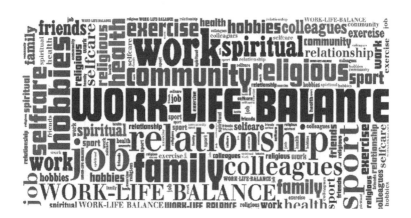

*YOUR RELATIONSHIP TO WORK*

# CHAPTER 5
## So You're Leaving Work?

### SOME THINGS TO CONSIDER:

• Are you retiring because you want to or because you assume that it is only natural to retire?

• What is it about work that you will miss the most?

*This chapter pushes you on the reasons that you are leaving work and how you feel about your job or career.* Ultimately, the reason why you leave work may have a big impact on how you view retirement. We want to make sure that you aren't just accepting retirement as a natural end to your work career and that you are clear about what you are leaving and what you are moving to in retirement.

I recently spoke with Allan, the mayor of our local community and owner of a dry cleaners. Allan was well known and respected in our community and had been for over 30 years. Allan was turning 65, his term as mayor was up, and he figured he would sell his business.

When I asked Allan why he is retiring even though he loved what he did and was much admired, Allan just sighed and said, "well, it's probably time. I am hitting 65 now and haven't really given any time to my wife or family. I have a vacation home down in Gulf Shores that I never get to and places around the world that I should see."

Clearly, Allan gave me the impression that he actually didn't want to quit what he was doing; in fact, he used the words "it's time" several times during our conversation.

### So You're Leaving Work

It sounds pretty attractive, doesn't it? Just think: no more having to get up in the morning when you don't want to and looking forward to weekends as a break from work, because now every day is going to be Saturday.

Most retiring boomers are very clear about what they are retiring *from*. Unfortunately, they are not always clear about what they are retiring *to*. The notion of retirement has always been presented as such a gift, a rite of passage and deliverance from the yoke of the workplace. In fact, many romanticize the idea of retiring and treat the idea of not working as the ultimate reward.

The dictionary defines work as "exertion or effort directed to produce or accomplish something; labour; toil." In our society, work is seen by many as a negative thing that has ruled much of our adult lives. The idea of retiring from work and "never having to work again" is at the foundation of a lot of retirement dreams.

But these days, people like Allan with his work-free retirement vision, are being overshadowed by those with a new view of retirement. *Research conducted by the American Association of Retired Persons (AARP) suggests that:*

• Eight in 10 baby boomers plan to work at least part-time "in retirement."
• Five per cent anticipate working full-time at a new job or career.
• Only 16% say they will not work at all.
• A 2013 survey by NORC Center for Public Affairs Research found that 47% of working Americans over 50 plan to delay retirement for at least three years, from age 63 until 66, and 82% of those surveyed said they expect to have to work for some income even after they retire.
What are you going to miss most about work?

*Planning a successful transition requires you to be completely honest with the significance of work in your life. When work is no longer your major endeavour, seek out ways to replace the contribution it makes to your life.*

— **Marion Haynes**

Depending on our experiences in the workplace, we all reframe our views of "work" and "retirement" in different ways. Positive perceptions of work may be associated with negative perceptions of retirement and vice versa.

*There are four main factors that may dictate how you feel about leaving work and entering retirement:*

**1 Unfinished business at work:** You may be involved in projects that have engaged you and are not yet completed. You may be excited about new opportunities that have arisen and view retirement as an end to your enthusiasm. However, you may feel that work has no positive rewards for you anymore and that there is nothing left to finish.

**2 Job satisfaction:** You may love what you do at work; in fact you live for it! Now you contemplate walking away from one of the things in life that gives you the most enjoyment. Or you may get no satisfaction from what you do and probably haven't been challenged for a long time.

**3 Financial situation:** You have a sense of financial comfort in the workplace, and are used to getting a steady paycheck, bonuses or commission. You know that you don't have to worry about maintaining your lifestyle as long as you have a job. On the other hand, you may feel that you have more than enough money to walk away and since you don't get anything out of work anyway, why not retire?

**4 Health:** You feel good, and you get a lot of energy from your work. You feel you could keep going for a long time because age is just a state of mind. On the flip side, you may no longer feel well enough to continue to work and are starting to feel older than your years.

We tend to reframe our view of *work* and *retirement* based on our experiences in these areas. As you look at your work, how do you feel about what you get out of the workplace?

"But why would I want to do that?" asked Mary, a 54-year-old schoolteacher in the Midwest who is anxious to get out of the classroom. "The fact is that I don't like to work, period, and I have spent far too long in a stressful environment that has robbed me of my desire to do anything further."

Mary is typical of a lot of pre-retirees who have focused on their retirement as a release from a stressful or unsatisfying career. They know what they don't like about the workplace and, while they still haven't settled on a vision of what their retirement will look like, they feel that "Anything beats working!"

"I know that retirement is on the horizon," said 60-year-old Joel in one of our interviews. "The problem that I have is that I don't really look forward to not having a place to go or things to do in retirement. Everyone else seems to be so excited about leaving work, but I really like what I do".

## Why Are You Retiring?

Why are you retiring from your present situation? There is no right or wrong answer: most Americans have careers that come to an end, whether by their choice or their company's. Often, that date is tied to a pension plan or an age-related number of years they have worked in a given position. Maybe their reason for going is that they have enough financial security so that they believe that they will "never have to work again."

Many boomers underestimate the importance of work because they focus on the prize at the end of the rainbow. It is easy to "demonize" our work because we have always been taught that retirement is a form of deliverance from the yoke of our work. People who enjoyed their work find themselves walking away for no reason other than "It's time!"

The traditional view of retirement held several justifications for leaving work. These, however, are irrelevant for many baby boomers.

## Do You Retire Because You Are Old?

If you are in good health, whether male or female, you can expect to live well into your late 80s.

The picture of what it means to be old has changed considerably. If you want to compare apples to apples, look at the relationship between longevity and retirement age used back in 1935 when the U.S. passed the Social Security Act. Accordingly, the retirement age for men today should not be 65, but in the late 80s.

We aren't old at age 65, and we certainly are not like previous generations. Author Gail Sheehy notes that "today's 50 is yesterday's 40." As a result, our concept of "old" has been reworked. That doesn't necessarily mean that we are all in any better shape than our parents, but many of us refuse to believe that we are closer to death than we are to Woodstock!

## Do You Retire Because You Can No Longer Contribute?

It may have once been true that you retired when you could no longer contribute. In those days, you were paid only for what you did. In today's knowledge society, however, many Americans also get paid for what they know.

Experience counts and is valued by many companies. One of the big crises faced by businesses is the loss of a tremendous bank of experience as baby boomers get set to leave the workforce. For example, it is estimated that more than 35% of American teachers are now over the age of 45.

A study on the challenge of retaining older workers found that many Americans could have been persuaded to stay at work. More than 25% of people who retired between 2002 and 2012 said they would have continued working had they been able to reduce their work schedule, either by working fewer days or by working shorter days, without their pensions being affected.

Similarly, 28% would have continued working if they had been offered part-time employment. About 27% might have been tempted to keep working if their health had been better, while 21% would have stayed if their salaries had been increased, although they were not asked by how much.

## Do You Retire Because You Want To Enjoy Our Golden Years?

Everyone likes a long weekend. Wouldn't it be nice to enjoy a 30-year-long weekend? If our golden years were defined as that time in our lives when we could put our feet up and watch the sunsets, wouldn't we want to relax for that length of time? As we will see later, the "paradox of leisure" is that if we have leisure 24 hours a day forever, where is our break?

And that's the problem. We have been trained to equate leisure with happiness, forgetting that many value leisure because it is a break from what we normally do. For example, we look forward to holidays because they give us a chance to do what we want, when we want. We are free from the demands of our jobs and can pursue our own interests.

## How Do You *Feel* About All Of This?

• Does this change the way that you view work and retirement?

• Can you see the possible benefits of working in retirement?

• Is your view of retirement one of leisure or one of opportunity?

# Exercise

## The Reason That I Am Retiring Is:

_____

_____

_____

_____

_____

## In Viewing Your Current Work, How Would You Rate Your Enjoyment Of What You Do?

*In the exercise below, we will give you an opportunity to think about the role that work plays and how you actually view leaving it.*

| 1 | 2 | 3 | 4 | 5 |
|---|---|---|---|---|
| I get no satisfaction whatsoever | Most of my time at work is unfulfilling | My work has both positive and negative effects on me | I get a lot of satisfaction from what I do | I can't wait to get to work each day |

## Having A Generally Negative View Of Work

If you rated your current view of work between 1 and 3, check off any of the reasons listed below that relate to why you are looking forward to retirement:

- ☐ Work is an obligation that I would rather not have.
- ☐ I find my work to be very stressful.
- ☐ Work is a source of personal or professional frustration.
- ☐ I am bored with what I am doing.
- ☐ I find my job to be too physically challenging.
- ☐ Work forces me to regiment my life.
- ☐ Work takes time away from my family and the things I like to do.
- ☐ Work forces me to think and I don't like that.
- ☐ I find work to be too difficult for me now.
- ☐ My workplace treats me with disrespect.

**What did you learn?** How many of the statements you checked above are specific to your current job? How many represent your views about work in general? How many could be fixed if you changed your focus, changed your career or started your own business?

## Having A Generally Positive View Of Work

If you rated your view of your current work between 3 and 5 in the above exercise, check off any of the reasons listed below that relate to why you are considering working in your retirement years. What particular aspects of work do you value the most?

- ☐ I like the idea of keeping busy.
- ☐ Work is a source of personal or professional satisfaction.
- ☐ Work allows me to be me.
- ☐ I really enjoy what I do.
- ☐ I don't find my job to be too physically challenging.
- ☐ Work gives structure to my life.
- ☐ Work gives me added income for me to do the things I like to do.
- ☐ Work keeps my mind active.
- ☐ My workplace treats me with respect.

**What did you learn?** As you examine the statements you checked above, how many are specific to your current job or represent your views on work in general? Pick the top three that you'd keep if you changed your focus, changed your career or started your own business.

# CHAPTER 6
## The Role That Work Plays In Your Life

## SOME THINGS TO CONSIDER:

- What does "going to work" mean to you?
- Do you think about your work constantly?
- Do you feel that your sense of self-worth is tied to your work?

There is a tendency to demonize work in order to make retirement look even more attractive. *In this chapter, we look at the value that work provides.* The goal is to look at it objectively without consideration of retirement. Work performs a basic function in our lives; we will look at the positives and consider whether we can take anything useful into retirement.

Robert, age 62, recently retired from a career as a civil engineer. From the time he was in college, he valued himself as an innovative thinker and builder who took on tough challenges and developed solutions. Over time, he moved to the top of his profession and worked as a consultant to both private industry and government. "Going to work every day wasn't really like going to work," he told us. "I looked forward to new challenges and creating unique ways to accomplish tough engineering tasks."

A health challenge caused Robert to retire long before he was ready to do so. Today, he still tries to keep up with new research and advances in engineering and has retained many friends through the Association of Professional Engineers.

"It's still not the same," he laments. "I feel that I have lost my relevance, my spark. I never realized how important my work was to how I see myself as a vital person."

## Your Identity And Your Work

It is easy to say that men tend to identify themselves by their work while women are more likely to identify themselves by their roles. Cultural anthropologists suggest that a man's historical role was that of a hunter and a gatherer and that his sense of self-worth came from his success versus other hunters. Women, on the other hand, created and maintained the social community needed to support the hunters.

Today, with so many women in the workplace, is there still a gender difference? In fact, the research on gender differences is not conclusive: both men and women who are fulfilled by their work are more likely to judge their self-worth by their jobs. If you don't have your job, who are you?

## Six Positive Roles That Work Plays In Your Life

Work provides positive benefits in your life that will need to be replaced if you decide that you never want to be employed again. There are six key roles that work plays:

**1** **Work provides you with a paycheck**
This is the most common reason that Americans work and what forces them to save for retirement. How important is your income to your lifestyle, your goals and dreams, and to your family? Does that paycheck ensure your quality of life? How secure is the paycheck that you currently receive? If your answers indicate that your paycheck plays a major role in the quality of your life, you will want to ensure that you truly understand your income flow and your income needs once you retire.

**2** **Work provides structure for your life**
One overlooked role that work fills in your life is the structure and purpose it creates in your weekly and daily activities. The workplace is a source of deadlines, starting times, lunch breaks, weekends and holidays. From the time you started your job, you were expected to be somewhere at a certain time to provide the services for which you were paid. The very nature of the workplace, with its ongoing deadlines and expectations, provides a certain amount of structure for your use of time—even if you are self-employed.

**3** **Work gives you a sense of "being needed"**
For some people, one of work's greatest benefits is that it fulfills a need to feel useful or helpful to others. Work can also provide a needed sense of accomplishment—knowing your work is directly benefiting someone and

that you have used your efforts for the greater good. While not all jobs are so altruistic, many do allow workers to combine their work with the values that they hold.

## 4 Work supplies your social network

Some people find that the workplace provides their support network, feeds their social life and, in some cases, replaces or supplements their family. Do you work because you enjoy the camaraderie at your job? How important are the personal relationships that have developed through your work? Work often supplies you with the type of team environment that fosters conversation and collaboration with colleagues to achieve common goals. And it is often these social and interactive aspects we appreciate as we reflect on our jobs at the end of the day.

## 5 Work offers you status

Depending on your job and how you view your position in life, your work may enhance your sense of self-worth. Your earning power may also translate into a feeling of personal power. Some people define themselves by their jobs and do not have a good sense of who they are without that identifier.

## 6 Work involves you in the community

When you go to work, you have a chance to interact with people in your community, to share ideas, to talk politics, sports, social issues, etc. In going to and from work, you are exposed to traffic, transportation modes and a view of the route between home and work. You can be drawn more easily into social causes, social activities within your community or receive recommendations on things to do.

**"About your retirement, Harry. I've just received a letter from your wife - she says she will pay your salary if we keep you on."**

*Retirement kills more people than hard work ever did.*

— **Malcolm S. Forbes**, *publisher*

# Exercise

## What Are The Positive Roles or Benefits That Work Plays In Your Life?

Review the six roles that work plays in your life below and rank them from 1-5 according to their relative importance to you, with 1 being the most important.

| Work provides you with… | Which means… | Rank how important this is to you |
|---|---|---|
| 1. Financial stability | The ability to contribute financially to your lifestyle and sustain it | |
| 2. Time management and structure | The structure provided through the expectations and time demands of your job | |
| 3. Sense of utility | The sense of purpose that work gives you and the motivation to improve | |
| 4. Social | The camaraderie that you feel with co-workers and the friends that you connect with at work | |
| 5. Status | The ego boost and sense of identity and accomplishment that satisfying employment gives you | |
| 6. Community | Getting out into the world and participating in situations as a result of your work | |

**What did you learn?** If you look at each work benefit, you can identify quickly which one was a major driver for you. In fact, you may have two or more drivers. As you plan for the future, which of these will you try to incorporate into your new life?

*Retirement at 65 is ridiculous. When I was 65, I still had pimples.*

— **George Burns,** *comedian and actor*

# CHAPTER 7
## What Are Your Strengths And Skills At Work?

### SOME THINGS TO CONSIDER:

• What strengths and skills do you have that could be transferred to another job or retirement interest (whether paid or not)?

• How will you replace the things you liked most about work?

• What strategies do you have to be actively engaged in society if you are not working?

• Now that you have choice, what job opportunities might appeal to you (whether paid or not)?

We all have things we feel we are better at than most other people. Often, we get the opportunity to use our strengths and skills when we are at work. Sometimes those may lead to advancement; other times, they just make us feel good about our accomplishments. If this is the case for you, then it is important to identify just what those strengths and transferable skills are so that you can find ways to use them in your Second Life.

### Making 'Work' A Part Of Your Retirement Life

In an earlier chapter, we examined the role that stress plays in retirement. A common stressor that may hit as you face retirement is the loss of one or more of the positive roles that work has played in your life. For example, the loss of a regular paycheck is an obvious stressor if your financial picture in retirement is not as solid as you might like.

Consider how the roles or functions of work have benefited you, and then explore activities and functions that you could substitute when "work" is no longer part of your experience.

## Financial Stability

Review your financial plan for this next phase of life and reconcile it with the life that you choose to live. Are you aware of the pension benefits that your company may have? Talk to your Human Resources professional at work or your financial advisor to discuss the options available to you. If you are a member of a stock option plan or you own company stock, make sure that you let your advisor know. With this information in hand, he or she will gain a more accurate picture of your total financial situation and provide you with appropriate advice.

Have you set aside enough money to enjoy your life or will you continually be concerned about whether you "have enough" for the future? You may want to consider ways to take a "graduated" retirement by job-sharing or working part-time if money is an issue.

The Society for Human Resource Management found that 25% of companies have developed strategies for older workers to work in new ways, including reduced hours. Another 24% plan to develop this type of working arrangement to accommodate seniors in the future.

One of the reasons that people look to retirement is that chronic health conditions make it harder to work. However, there is also a large group of Americans who have chosen to continue their work despite physical limitations.

## Time Management and Structure

Successful retirees normally try to add some elements of structure to their lives that once existed in their workplace. Don't shy away from commitments or obligations. Go ahead! Create plans and develop short-term goals and strategies to achieve them.

## Utility and Value

If you have a need to "be needed," your retirement is a great time to volunteer in your community or to take on part-time work where your efforts will be appreciated by someone else. Charities and other non-profit organizations are always on the lookout for people willing to contribute their time and energy. Pick an organization that is in keeping with your values and then find out how you can help in ways that fit with your skills and desires.

## Community

If your work is the source of your social life, try to expand your friendships outside of the workplace. This is a good opportunity to get involved with other organizations to meet people and form new associations. Also, make sure that you put in extra effort to transfer your significant work friendships to your new life.

Often it is assumed that work friendships will automatically survive retirement. When people get busy with their lives, however, it is too easy for these valuable friendships to slip away—more from lack of attention than from a lack of desire.

## Status

If your sense of self-worth is enhanced because of your job, try to find ways to take on roles in your retirement that will continue to provide you with the reinforcement you need. Many retired executives volunteer with not-for-profit organizations, or involve themselves in fund-raising or political campaigns, or sit on corporate boards or community committees. Replacing the status gained from the workplace is perhaps the toughest obstacle to overcome for many high-powered executives. The solution is to identify the need for status as an issue and then to use the time remaining until retirement to redefine yourself in a way that allows you to transition into retirement without longing for the position that you no longer hold.

## Forward Progress

Get a jump on a new career by going back to school—either part-time or full-time. You won't be alone!
The ability to learn is not related to how young you are. In fact, you may find yourself feeling re-energized by the challenges and opportunities that open up on campus. There are many stories of the 50-plus sophomore revelling in the idealism of his or her twentysomething classmates.

## What Are Your Strengths And Transferable Skills?

It is so easy to think of the negative aspects of your work and forget the things that you liked to do when you were there! We all have things that we feel we do better than most and often we can exercise those skills in the workplace.

As you move into your retirement, consider those skills that you applied to work and that often would brighten your day or give you satisfaction because you felt that you were contributing something of yourself. These are transferable to your retirement and can provide you with ideas on:

- New full or part-time employment
- Teaching or consulting opportunities
- Hobbies
- Personal education
- Coaching, mentoring

## Taking Work Into Retirement

Companies such as HSBC, Marriott Hotels, Disney and Walmart have programs to hire older workers to replace the twentysomething staff who use service jobs as stepping stones to other careers.

A generation ago, it could be said that there was no room for an older worker in the workforce. Today, many corporations are concerned about losing their most experienced employees to retirement and are actively working on ways to allow them to stay active in a way that best suits the employee. And, as baby boomers age and the generations behind them don't have the numbers to fill the needed jobs in the workforce, it is likely that companies will become more creative about finding ways to keep older boomers in the workforce.

## Work Redefined In Your Retirement

I ran into a retired lawyer when I was recently on holidays in California. He had always wanted to become a winemaker, so when he left his law practice, he bought a small vineyard in the Santa Barbara area. He told me he was working 10 to 12 hours a day, but that he absolutely loved it! "My father used to remind me of that old adage, 'If you love what you do, you never have to work again!' This isn't work for me, but it is the foundation of this great new life that I have chosen."

A wise person once said, "If you love what you do, you never have to work again!" With that in mind, a good definition of your "work" might be: *Any time you are using your talents, experience, time or wisdom for the benefit of others, you are working*. With that definition, it is easier to look forward to work.

One of the opportunities open to you in this next phase of life is to discover what you really love to do and then find a way to build your future around it. If you need income, your plan will need to include how to best earn money doing what you love to do, whether that's working for a new employer, starting your own business, working part-time for someone else or consulting.

As you make your plans for the future, consider the role that work could play in your longevity, your life fulfillment and your activity level. If you decide that work should be very much a part of the next phase of your life, then you will want to spend some time reflecting on what kinds of things you might like to do. This will help you choose the work that will allow you to be involved in the activities that are of greatest interest to you.

It is important to examine the role that work plays in your life today, including your strengths and skills, and the ideal work situation that will suit your vision of your retirement life.

## What Are Your Work Options in Retirement?

Some important questions to ask are "What are the positive impacts on my life from staying in the workforce?" and "What is the 'good stuff' I get from being employed?"

Even if you are really looking forward to retirement, is there something about your work that you will miss? Consider any positive effects of your job on your life—will they be missing if you just "walked away"?
*Here are some of your choices:*

### 1 Traditional Retirement

This is the retirement that many have promised themselves since they first started working. For many, it means completely leaving the workplace and pursuing a life of fun activities as you enjoy your golden years. It offers the opportunity to use the time that you are not spending at work to pursue your other interests, hobbies etc. Since this definition is really "work vs. no work," ask yourself these questions:

> • If I won the lottery and money was not an issue, what is it about work that I would miss the most?
>
> • Do I truly look at work as a negative, or is there a positive definition that I might put on it as I plan for traditional retirement? In other words, is traditional retirement what I really want, or do I just want to stop doing what I am doing now?
>
> • Do I have any choices regarding my retirement date, or can I find a way to continue doing what I like to do (part-time, job-sharing, etc.)?

### 2 Graduated Retirement

More aging workers would like to combine work and leisure and are considering a "phased-in" retirement that includes arrangements such as working part-time, taking on a consulting role or job-sharing. In some cases, they may take partial pensions while still contributing in some way to employers and to their own paychecks by staying involved. *There are a couple of reasons why you might choose graduated retirement:*

- You still need the money (either don't want or can't afford full retirement).
- You are still needed in your job and have made an arrangement with your employer to begin pulling back.

If you are looking at graduated retirement as a way of "having your cake and eating it too," you are not alone. Many baby boomers are considering ways to stay involved, and human resource departments across North America are developing unique ways to keep the older workers in the workplace.

## 3 Semi-Retirement

This is similar to graduated retirement, but is more commonly a retirement strategy for self-employed individuals. The key to enjoying semi-retirement appears to be the control that you have over your time. There is an assumption that you can afford to be semi-retired and that you can call your own shots on how you spend your time.

## 4 Reverse Retirement

One recent demographic phenomenon is the concept of "reverse retirement" to describe the return to the workforce of previously retired individuals. Jack Singh is a 63-year-old retired sales manager who has recently come back into the workforce. "When I retired three years ago, I had the idea that I would keep myself busy and not have to worry about how I spent my time. After a year of driving my wife nuts, I decided for the good of our marriage that I should take advantage of an offer to join some old friends in a consulting company. I get to choose the projects that I want to work on and it enables me to use all of my knowledge in my own field while not totally walking away from retirement."

A Cornell University retirement and well-being study found that 89% of retirees who returned to work in "reverse retirement" did so because they "wanted to keep active." *Some of the other reasons listed were:*

- "Had the free time"
- "Maintain social contacts"
- "Desired additional income"

An increasing number of Americans are returning to the workforce after retirement. Interestingly, financial security is not the main reason: many cite "boredom" or "to take advantage of an interesting opportunity."

That trend is expected to continue as many early retirees reassess their long-term work goals due to adopting better health practices, needing to maintain a lifestyle, having a younger outlook on life and realizing that they may have had a misunderstanding about the allure of continuous leisure.

## 5 No Retirement

Many Americans refuse to leave the workplace because they love to be involved. Consider the 80 year old who continues to go to the office every day and refuses to stop. His work is the highlight of his day.

The statistics for men and women working past age 65 are roughly the same, although women are more likely to undertake part-time work while men opt for full-time. Seventy per cent of women expect to work after age 66 because of financial need, while men are much more likely to work in later life out of choice.

## A Second Career?

Developing a second career to augment retirement income is quite common today, but it takes planning and time to develop new networks. The following steps can help you explore possibilities for a second career:

• Create a new personal mission statement. Write down a wish list of jobs that fit your mission and your life's purpose.

• Review your list while considering your set of unique skills, talents and strengths.

• Shorten the list to four or five possibilities.

• Reach out to meet people who are working in the jobs or fields you have on your list, or talk to those people who run the type of business you'd like to start.

• Shorten your list to a few possibilities and investigate each of these in depth, including requirements such as an advanced or new college degree or even individual courses that might be relevant.

*It is seldom that one retires from business to enjoy his fortune in comfort…*
*he works because he has always worked, and knows no other way!*
— **Thomas Nichols**

# Exercise

## Self-Discovery: Your Strengths and Transferable Skills

Think of the things that you really like about work, those things that create positive energy for you.

- Leading
- Teaching
- Public Speaking
- Delegating
- Team Building
- Listening
- Managing
- Politicking
- Implementing
- Creating
- Consulting
- Learning

- Analyzing
- Strategizing
- Calculating
- Problem-Solving
- Designing
- Tinkering or Building
- Editing
- Planning
- Selling
- Simplifying
- Coordinating
- Creating

- Relationships
- Organizing
- Writing
- Mentoring
- Facilitating
- Building
- Boosting
- Morale
- Travelling
- Restructuring
- Physical Exertion

## What Can You Do?

In the previous exercise, you examined those things that you liked to do in your job. You were able to articulate your traits, skills or strengths that contributed to a positive work experience for you. Very often we are well aware of our weaknesses, sometimes to the point of being overcritical of ourselves. Many people are more comfortable (and familiar) with their weaknesses than they are with their strengths. They sometimes need help in developing a vocabulary of strengths and support in talking about them.

This next exercise is about building a picture of your personal strengths. In the space below you have room to make an exhaustive list of all of the things that you can do. Don't limit the list to work-related skills, but include your hobbies, life skills, talents, resources, strengths, capabilities and potentials of all kinds, even things that you haven't done for years!

# Exercise

## Skills, Talents, Abilities, Strengths, Capabilities…

I Can…

_____

_____

_____

_____

# Exercise

## Your Peak Work Experiences

Think back and select from your work experience one episode that stands out as a "peak" experience. This was an experience that gave you intense fulfillment, broke through the pattern of everyday life…you know what we're talking about. Select a specific event rather than a period of time. Focus on the _work moment_ rather than on the reward moment that might have followed. Think about it…visualize it…try to live it in every vivid detail. Where are you? What is the date and time? What led you to this moment? Who else is there? How do you feel? Are there any other circumstances you can remember?

| | Peak Experience | Skills, Talents and Abilities I used |
|---|---|---|
| 1 | | |
| 2 | | |
| 3 | | |
| 4 | | |
| 5 | | |

**What did you learn?** The tendency is for people to look at their last jobs and then find ways to replicate what they had recently enjoyed. This exercise encourages you to "think outside the box" and to go back to a time when you may have used other skills or were engaged in a completely different kind of work. For example, a retired accountant at a workshop now restores old cars because he worked as a mechanic when he was going to university. At a Home Depot seminar on deck building, the instructor had retired from a career in manufacturing and was now teaching homeowners about woodwork on Saturday mornings.

# Exercise

## Putting Together a Retirement Work Plan

As you consider the information that you wrote down from the preceding exercises, ask yourself what kind of work you might like to do in your next phase of life. Here is a questionnaire to help you organize the information:

The reason I am retiring is…

The thing I will miss most about work is…

The way that I will replace this in my retirement is…

In my life, the major role that work plays is…

The things I love to do at work are…

_____

_____

_____

_____

My ideal retirement work would be…

_____

_____

_____

_____

The strengths or skills that I have to do this are…

_____

_____

_____

_____

The steps that I need to take to build this new endeavour are…

_____

_____

_____

_____

A part-time work pursuit that I would like is…

_____

_____

_____

_____

The steps that I need to undertake to make this happen are…

_____

_____

_____

_____

# What Will You Do With This Information?

## DID YOU KNOW?

• Psychologists at the University of Maryland found that those who engaged in part-time work following retirement had improved physical health (lower blood pressure, less cancer and strokes) compared with those who stopped work altogether.

•A 2012 TD Economics Observation reports that since the jobs recovery began in mid-2009, individuals aged 60 and over have accounted for about one-third of all net new job gains.

• A September 2012 study says in June of last year over half a million Americans were involved in start ups (businesses less than two years old) and by far the fastest growing segment of the start-up market was the 50 and over age group.

# PART 3

*YOUR MIND IN RETIREMENT*

# CHAPTER 8
## Mentally Preparing To Retire

### SOME THINGS TO CONSIDER:

• Do you have the right "mindset" to get full enjoyment out of this next phase of your life?
• How well do you handle life's stresses and challenges today?
• Have you handled changes in your life in a positive way?
• Is retirement the end or the beginning for you?

In this chapter, we look at the role that your outlook plays in your retirement success or challenge. Retirement, or your Second Life, is more a sharpening of your mind than a change in your workplace. This is a time to figure out who you really are and then living the life that you want to live. Our point in this chapter is that to really self-actualize, you first have to understand what is important to you.

*The greatest discovery of my generation…is that human beings can alter their lives by altering their attitudes of mind.*

— **William James**, *psychologist and philosopher*

Bruce and Jitendra had planned for their retirement for about five years before Bruce was ready to leave his job as a school principal. Many of their friends were either retired or facing retirement and provided the couple with good examples of both what to do and not to do when it came to making the transition from a regular work life. "I was amazed at the number of my friends who reached their retirement and basically had no idea what they were going to do once they got there," Bruce commented. "Jitendra and I told ourselves that we were going to take this opportunity to get everything out of this new life—we were going to make it an adventure."

For the past five years, they have taken a month in the summer and "practised" retirement. "We were initially concerned that we might find it difficult to change our mindset once we actually retired," Jitendra said. "I knew from my work as a psychologist that making a major life change such as retiring is a lot more stressful than most people realize."

## Looking Inside Yourself

What is your mindset when you think of retirement?

Successful retirees are generally optimistic people who believe that they can control parts of their lives. They seek out new opportunities to learn or experience new things—they refuse to give in to an attitude that focuses on aging as negative or that retirement means being "near the end." The key is their attitude toward whatever life has dealt them, including their ability to control their attitude!

As we noted in the introduction, however, not everyone is the same. You may be reading this book and not feeling terribly optimistic. Please don't put it down! You do have some control over how you want to feel and can make some simple changes or slight adjustments to add enjoyment to your view of your retirement. Here is a great quote!

*If you are distressed by anything external, the pain is not due to the thing itself, but to your estimate of it; and this you have the power to revoke at any moment.*

—**Marcus Aurelius,** *Roman emperor*

## False Assumptions

Financial planning clients and their advisors often assume that there is a template for the "ideal" retirement—walking away from work with enough money to do all of those things that you always dreamt of doing when you never had enough time! This is one of the reasons why retirement planning often becomes a financial planning exercise. The false belief is that as long as you have enough money, you can happily retire.

The problem with that is that people focus on having enough money and ignore figuring out how they want to *feel* or *think*.

With this model in mind, many pre-retirees we talk to tend to see their retirement future as a series of weekends strung together over 30 years. In our workshops we advise participants that the keys to retirement success are actually no different than the keys to life success—i.e., the way you view yourself and your place in the world will determine whether you are able to maintain a happy retirement life.

**Roy:** *"I have now been retired from my job for nine months. The guys were asking me the other day how I like it and I told them that it was like having a continual holiday from work. I just love it. I can golf every day and no one tells me where I have to be or where I have to go. Actually, though, I've found that after six or seven days of golf in a row, I'm burnt out and I spend the next day on the couch. The other thing I notice is that I'm not using my mind very much and that I've got a nice spare tire around my waist. But those are the only negative things. Hey, I'm only 60 and I have a lot of time to work out all of the bugs in this retirement thing."*

Roy looked at his pending retirement as an opportunity to play golf. His planning had zeroed in on what he wanted to do, not on how he wanted to feel. While there is nothing wrong with creating a bucket list, remember that it is your outlook on life and the way that you look at the world that will drive activities, positive mental health, relationships, etc.

Retirement planning is more about conditioning your mind than taking an activity-centered approach.

## Who are you?

Often when we pose the question "who are you?" we will get responses ranging from "I am a lawyer" to "I am a manager" to "I work in manufacturing." Both men and women define themselves based on how they see their position in the world. There is no research that says that most men define themselves any differently than most women!

In setting your goals and priorities for this next phase of your life, it is a good idea to clarify the present roles that you feel you play as well as future roles that you wish to play. By understanding who you are and where your natural talents lie, it will be easier to decide where you want to go and how you want to spend your time in your Second Life. How do you see yourself today? What is your self-image? Which parts of you are most important to you?

In our exercise section of this chapter, we have included a great thought-provoker to help you identify who you really are!

## You Are Who You Are: Continuity Theory

"When we retire, we are going to do a lot of new things," Mary confided at our retirement seminar. "I have never painted before and I think that I can use my time to take art lessons and start painting." Her husband Bob was also excited about the new possibilities. "We have put down a list of all of the things we have always wanted to do, and our goal in retirement is to make sure that we do each and every one!"

That sounds both ambitious and exciting! There will be others who will be able to compile a  list of new things that will become part of their day-to-day lives as they move through the first stages of retirement. Whether Bob and Mary embark on new, exciting lives has more to do with whether they are "self-starters" or "other-directed" than whether they have more time.

To get a sense of your likelihood to do a lot of "new" things in retirement, look at whether you have done a lot of new things in the past! Some people continually look for adventure and are open to new opportunities; others will always find excuses or impediments to adding some zest or change.

Psychologists have used the term *continuity theory* to describe how we generally are consistent in our attitudes, beliefs, expectations and habits. The theory is based on the premise that human beings do not like change or dissonance in their lives; when we embark on something new or we change our situation, our brains find ways to restore normalcy.

The theory has also been applied to the natural process of aging. As we age, we keep the same personality, relationships and "our way of doing things"; the strategies that older adults use to process getting older are often rooted in their past experiences.

Simply put, you are who you are.

That doesn't necessarily mean that you won't do new things; it's just positive habits to undertake them. Generally, it doesn't "just happen" simply because you now have more time in retirement.

## Self-Starters And 'Other-Directed' People

*Everything you do is based on the choices you make. It's not your parents, your past relationships, your job, the economy, the weather, an argument or your age that is to blame. You and only you are responsible for every decision and choice you make.*

— **Dr. Wayne Dyer,** *American life coach*

Psychologists refer to whether we are "self-starters" or "other"-directed" people as based on our 'locus of control'. We also call this being "internally driven" versus "externally driven." In other words, it is a measure of our likelihood to feel that we have control over certain aspects of our lives versus whether we believe that we are powerless to control anything that happens to us.

Few of us are at the extremes of the spectrum; most of us are somewhere in between. It has been suggested that our sense of feeling "in control" is related to our cognitive health, our feelings of well-being and our outlook for the future. In addition, the aging process naturally affects this sense of being self-directed. The older we get, the less likely we are to feel that we have the ability to impact our world and control it.

Research tells us that self-starters do better than other-directed people. For people who feel their locus of control is external rather than internal, there are ways to move more toward taking charge of your life.

*Here are the keys to becoming more self-directed:*

- ✔ Feel good about who you are
- ✔ Have a clear vision of where you want to go in the key areas of your life
- ✔ Respect yourself and your ideas
- ✔ Take other people's counsel, but undertake to make your decisions yourself
- ✔ Recognize that you create your own reality, both positive and negative

You may start your retirement by considering yourself self-directed, but you may feel more powerless as you age. This process normally starts around age 50! However, successful retirees understand how important it is to stay positive and to appreciate the power they have to change the course of their lives.

We have used the term "positive psychology" several times in this book to describe how the mind can positively affect retirement success. Our discussion of the "hardy personality," retirement happiness, optimism and feeling in control are all key elements. Abraham Maslow first used the term in the forties 1940s *(see Chapter 2)* and is directly tied to the concept of self-actualization in his 'needs' pyramid.

## The Importance Of Optimism

If you feel positive about the future, you can't wait for the day to begin—after all, there are new ways to explore, laugh, love and enjoy. Optimists look at the bright side of most situations and are able to make lemonade out of lemons.

Optimism means that you see your world as being the way that it should be and that the future will unfold in a similar fashion. Optimism is an element of positive psychology, formulated by Dr. Martin Seligman; in chapter 9, we will look at Seligman's concept of PERMA as a description of happiness. One of the drivers of PERMA is optimism. For more information on PERMA and happiness, see chapter nine.

Optimists see challenges as stepping stones to final positive solutions. Pessimists, on the other hand, see obstacles as permanent. That reinforces the other-directed personality—individuals who look for impediments to success and feel little control over their ability to make things happen.

There will be many challenges in retirement. If you are an optimist, you will find ways to reframe your obstacles into something that can be positive over the long run.

*Consider these challenges in retirement and the optimist's response:*

**Health:** Optimists believe that they should do whatever they can to control their health. After that, they manage the transition to a new reality.

*Relationships:* Optimists avoid conflict and manage discord without creating animosity. Things that are harmful to relationships, such as gossip, jealousy or envy, are not part of an optimist's personality.

*Financial security:* Optimists control what they can control and ignore the things that they can't. As part of managing to create financial security, optimists plan for the things that they want to accomplish and protect themselves from things that may harm them.

*Aging:* Optimists tend to see aging as validating their human life and part of the natural course of things. Again, they control what they can control and accept the things they can't.

*Bereavement:* Optimists understand that they cannot change what has happened. This doesn't mean that they don't grieve, but they also transition into their new reality with the view that "Today is the first day of the rest of my life."

*Retirement from work:* Optimists may move from their previous jobs to seek a new experience or enter a new phase of their lives. They will often take the positives from their previous work lives and try to use that in their new lives.

"What's with Terrence?"

## Optimists May Live Longer

In a study of more than 100,000 women since 1954, researchers looked at the effects on life and health of an optimistic personality. After eight years of follow-up, they found that women who were optimistic—those who expect good rather than bad things to happen—were 14% less likely to die from any cause than pessimists and 30% less likely to die from heart disease.

Optimists also were also less likely to have high blood pressure or diabetes, or to smoke cigarettes.

## Exercise

### Who Am I?

The exercise below is a valuable one that has been used by psychologists for a long time. We use it in retirement planning because it gives you a snapshot of how you see yourself today and in the future.

In this exercise, you will explore your personal view of who you really are. You will want to free-associate in order to get the most from it. Don't censor anything and quickly write down whatever comes to mind.

Write down a series of statements about yourself after the words **I AM**…

Your statements could reflect any aspect of your life: your job, your relationships, etc.

*For example:*

> **I am** a father, husband, sister, daughter, friend, collaborator, and problem-solver.
> **I am** a caregiver, community volunteer, boss, executive, lawyer, etc.
> **I am** intelligent, caring, loved, respected.

I am

I am

I am

I am

I am

I am

I am

I am

I am

I am

I am

I am

I am

Now discard the five that are least important, and then prioritize the remaining in order of importance to you now and in your Second Life. Then, for each role you listed, list what you love about that part of your identity and then list the talents you bring to that role.

*For example:*

**I am a:** *problem-solver.*

**What I love about this role is:** *Collaborating with others and generating a positive creative energy to find practical solutions that work!*

**The talents that I bring to this role are:** *My ability to find common ground, my can-do attitude, my interpersonal and problem-solving skills and my* *practical nature that seeks to keep things simple and doable.*

What common threads do you see in your answers to the "**Who Am I?**" activity? How do you see yourself today and what roles and talents do you want to carry with you to use to the fullest during the next phase of your

| I Am A... | What I Love About This Role Is... | The Talents That I Bring To This Role Are... |
|---|---|---|
|  |  |  |
|  |  |  |
|  |  |  |
|  |  |  |
|  |  |  |

# Exercise

## How Prepared Are You Mentally For Retirement?

In the exercise below, we have given you two sets of statements. These represent opposite ends of the spectrum in each area. In the middle is a column that represents "somewhere in the middle" that you can tick if neither choice applies. Remember the bell curve that we talked about earlier. Are you closer to one side or in the middle?

| If you are *externally* driven | | Neutral | | If you are *internally* driven |
|---|---|---|---|---|
| Retirees are happy doing what they do and don't seek to change anything. | I don't generally try new things. | | I am always trying new things. | Successful retirees tend to be open to new challenges and pursuits. |
| Retirees try to maintain the status quo where possible. | I don't like a lot of change in my life. | | I embrace change and make the best of it. | Retirement is a time of great change. Successful retirees make adjustments to their new situation. |
| Retirees tend to focus on flow activities and are content with the journey rather than the destination. | I have a few things that I like to do in my spare time. | | I have lots of things that I like to do in my spare time. | Successful retirees try to create a balance between many different kinds of activities. |
| Retirees make their surroundings fit their needs and find comfort in what they have. | I would never consider changing where I live. | | I would be open to changing where I live if the circumstances are right. | Successful retirees adjust to their changing reality, even if it means moving to a new home; those who will not change may find that change is forced on them by health or family circumstances that they didn't anticipate. |
| Retirees focus on feeling well mentally. | I don't exercise regularly. | | I like to exercise regularly. | One of the keys to healthy aging is to find time regularly to raise your heart rate or to regularly exercise. Those who live a sedentary lifestyle may encounter health challenges that will compromise their life enjoyment. |

| *externally* driven ...continued | | Neutral | | *internally* driven ...continued |
|---|---|---|---|---|
| Retirees are happy with who they are or are prepared to accept their situation. | I don't pay attention to good health principles. | | I pay a lot of attention to good health principles. | Understanding the principles of healthy aging includes both mental and physical health awareness. Failing to pay attention to the basic principles of healthy aging may compromise longevity or retirement happiness. |
| Retirees are sceptical about the advice they receive and worry often about the safety of their money. | I am usually concerned about my finances. | | I am seldom concerned about my finances. | Successful retirees are normally comfortable with their financial situation and have an understanding of the extent of the financial resources available to them. Concern over one's financial situation can affect life enjoyment by creating unnecessary stress or missed opportunities. |
| Retirees don't feel the need for new friendships and may have a few close friends. | I don't have a big social network. | | I have a large social network. | Saving in retirement should not be undertaken at the expense of lifestyle enjoyment or health. Successful retirees find balance and try to use their money to invest for the future and provide lifestyle enjoyment today. |
| Retirees are concerned with the return of their money, not getting a return on their money. | I tend to be more of a saver. | | I want my money to work as hard as it can for me. | Successful retirees continue to expand their social network and recognize the value of strong and nurturing friendships. A limited social network can lead to stress and a sense of isolation in later life. |

| externally driven ...continued | Neutral | | internally driven ...continued |
|---|---|---|---|
| Retirees are not outgoing or social and see no need to build a social network. | I don't make friends easily. | I make friends easily. | The key to expanding a social network is the willingness to meet new people and create new personal relationships. Those retirees who have trouble meeting new people and creating commonality will likely see their social networks shrink over time. |
| Retirees don't find comfort in their families. | My immediate family causes me much anxiety. | My immediate family is a source of much comfort and fun. | In retirement, close family relationships become increasingly important to mental and physical health; those without nurturing family relationships may experience loneliness and isolation. |
| Retirees have a limited social network of nurturing and supporting friends. | I don't have many close, supportive ongoing relation-ships. | I enjoy several close, supportive, ongoing relationships with good friends. | There is a direct correlation between the existence of an intimate relationship and longevity. |
| Retirees believe that work is a negative and that leisure is an ideal situation. | I dislike my work. | I love my work. | Current dissatisfaction with work may affect how a retiree views work in general. Successful retirees tend to look at work as a positive and seek out opportunities to use work as positive mental stimulation. |

| *externally* driven<br>...*continued* | | *Neutral* | | *internally* driven<br>...*continued* |
|---|---|---|---|---|
| Retirees are not content with doing something over and over and have fewer interests that engage them. | I get bored easily. | | I am seldom bored. | Successful retirees make good use of their time, balancing out both fulfilling and time-filling activities. Boredom and lack of purpose leads to stress and can compromise both mental and physical health. |
| Retirees are not content with doing something over and over and have fewer interests that engage them. | I get bored easily. | | I am seldom bored. | Successful retirees make good use of their time, balancing out both fulfilling and time-filling activities. Boredom and lack of purpose leads to stress and can compromise both mental and physical health. |
| Retirees believe that stress is something that is always there and find themselves distressed often about normal life events or perceived catastrophes. | I carry a lot of stress in my life. | | Stress is not a big factor in my life. | The No. 1 cause of death in both American men and women is stress-related disease, such as cardio-vascular, stroke or stress-related cancers. The ability to manage stress will be an important factor in a happy and contented retirement. |
| Retirees equate their view of themselves with their "work persona." | My work position means a lot to me. | | My work position doesn't mean a lot to me. | If you tend to define yourself by your job, you will have to redefine yourself when you retire. Successful retirees find replacements for the things that they liked about work, but their identity and sense of self-worth is not tied to their position at work. |

| externally driven ...continued | | Neutral | | internally driven ...continued | |
|---|---|---|---|---|---|
| Retirees don't believe that structure is important and that retirement should mean "no structure." | I don't like structure in my life. | | I like a lot of structure in my life. | Successful retirees understand that structure has always been part of their lives and that, in retirement, they will have to find ways to incorporate structure. Those without structure will likely find a retirement without purpose. | |
| Retirees believe that "whatever will happen will happen" and that they have no control over it. | I don't make a lot of plans for the future. | | I like to make plans for my future. | Creating an overall plan for the future makes handling the inevitable life transitions a lot easier. Those without a plan tend to lack goals or day-to-day structure in their lives that would lead to life enjoyment. | |
| Retirees are not motivated by achievement or success. | I don't have many things in my life that I consider achieve-ments. | | I have many things, big and small in my life that I consider to be achievements. | Successful retirees continue to strive for achievement and cherish victories both large and small. | |
| Retirees look at a "glass half-empty." | I consider myself a pessimist or realist. | | I consider myself to be an optimist. | Successful retirees are optimistic about the future and try to look at the positives in each situation. | |
| Retirees see no need to learn new things or engage in new activities. | I don't try to learn a lot of new things and feel that my education is basically over. | | I am always learning new things and continue to find ways to keep myself mentally active. | In retirement, you will have to "use it or lose it." Successful retirees continue to learn new things and to challenge themselves by undertaking new mental pursuits. There is a direct correlation between mental activity and longevity. | |

*Scoring This Exercise:*

Look at three things as you consider your responses:

**1.** How many check marks did you put on the left-hand column? Is there a reason why you have chosen to take that approach?

**2.** Consider the check marks that you put in the middle column. How much effort would it be to move more to the right column?

**3.** What specific things do you think you should do to incorporate the ideas in the far right-hand column into your retirement plan?

There are no right or wrong answers to the above statements. Not everyone is an extrovert or a self-starter and there are many retirees who are perfectly content in retirement even though they ticked off more items in the left-hand column.

## What Will You Do With This Information?

How can you use this to focus on being the person you really want to be in your Second Life?

Can you strengthen how you define yourself to reflect how you see yourself rather than how others see you?

Are you optimistic or pessimistic about the future? Don't confuse being a realist with being a pessimist—if you are a realist, you will try to control what you can and then understand that there are some things that are beyond your control. For example, you can't control certain elements of your health but you can always control how you feel about your health.

### DID YOU KNOW?

• People with internal locus of control are generally healthier emotionally and physically than those who have an external locus of control. (Glicken, 2010)

• When compared to people who feel powerless to control their lives, people with a sense of control know more about health, are more likely to initiate preventive behaviours such as quitting smoking, exercising or maintaining normal weight, and consequently have better self-rated health, fewer illnesses, and lower rates of mortality.
(Mirowsky and Ross, 2003)

# CHAPTER 9
## How Would You Define Retirement Happiness?

**SOME THINGS TO CONSIDER:**

• What does a happy retirement mean to you?

• What is it that will make you happy if you are not presently so?

• What is the role of money in retirement happiness?

• Is there science behind identifying the keys to retirement happiness?

In this chapter we will explore the keys to a happy retirement from a psychological perspective. Can retirement happiness really be quantified? What are its main elements and how can you strengthen yourself in each area? Finally, we look at whether it is possible to plan for your future happiness as you think about the future.

"When we retire, we are going to be so happy," Margaret told us at a workshop in Kansas City. "There are so many places that we want to visit and things we want to do. We are really looking forward to the beginning of our new life." Her husband Dave was more uncertain about the future. "I am not really sure how I am going to adjust," he said. "I know that Margaret has all sorts of plans, but frankly I am a little concerned about whether I even want to retire."

Margaret's view of the future clearly is different than the reality of the life she leads today. She is bored at home and now that the children are grown Margaret is ready for a change. "I really feel miserable at the moment, but the saving grace is our retirement," she told us. "We have both worked so long and not had the life that we wanted. Retirement for us will be a very happy time!"

## What Will Make You Happy In Your Second Life?

Philosopher Robin Sharma wrote, "Happiness is an action, not a result." Many people on the verge of their transition to retirement hope that the next phase of their lives will result in happiness. In fact, a lot of retirement planning focuses on how to achieve happiness in your golden years.

When you plan your retirement and decide that you will travel the world or that you will take up new activities, there is a tendency to associate your happiness with your ability to achieve these goals. People often will say, "When I am retired, I am going to be happy," or "When we don't have to work anymore we will be happy!"

Achieving your goals will certainly help you live a happy life, but happiness itself is not a goal: it is a precondition to living the life that you want. If you are miserable now, you will likely be miserable in retirement no matter how many trips you take!

## The "Rush-Crash" Phenomena

Elizabeth Mokyr Horner, PhD, of the University of California, Berkeley has done a lot of work in the area of retirement happiness. She has observed that many retirees tend to look forward to retirement and experience something that she calls a "sugar rush" immediately after retirement. However, this feeling of elation is often replaced by an emotional crash that can last for longer periods of time. In fact, Horner noted in her 2012 study in the Journal of Happiness Studies that this "rush-crash" phenomenon occurred regardless of what age the subject retired.

Many pre-retirees link happiness with the retirement event itself. Once they discover that retirement was not a destination rather than a transition they must change their expectations of happiness to fit their daily lives. Reframing the concept of retirement in this way can not only make the transition easier, but also can help avoid the crash of unfulfilled expectations.

Some try to spend their way out of the crash. Typically, spending patterns follow the initial rush; however, some retirees try to keep the magic happening by trying to add new excitement through money.

*It's not having what you want, it's wanting what you've got.*
—*singer* **Sheryl Crow**, *Soak Up the Sun*

## Can Retirement Happiness Be Quantified?

A common question that we receive is, "What are the keys to retirement happiness?" Many people are under the assumption that the concepts of happiness and financial security are inextricably combined.

In survey work conducted by The Retirement Lifestyle Center with both pre-retirees and retirees, approximately 75% of the pre-retirees surveyed said that the key to happiness was having enough money to enjoy their lives.

However, when we interviewed retirees, the overwhelming key was listed as "having good health." In fact, money was No. 4 with retirees, after "nurturing and supporting relationships" and "fulfilling activities."

A study in Canada on personal happiness found that people don't have to succeed in absolutely everything they do to feel happy. Happiness was related to feeling in control of their lives. In fact, those who believed that they were responsible for their own positions and decisions expressed one third more life satisfaction than those who did not.

Have you ever had a day where you didn't get enjoyment out of an activity that would normally really excite you? I am a dedicated golfer, but I have to confess that some days I would rather not be out on the golf course! When we forget why it is that we like doing the things that we do, they become empty activities.

Rather than simply throwing up our hands and saying that there is no one formula for retirement happiness, let's look at some of the latest research done in the area of positive psychology.

In studies conducted at the University of Pennsylvania, researchers found that there isn't just one key to a successful, happy retirement; they have identified the five keys that work in concert to contribute to an overall sense of peace, contentment and a living a successful life.

Led by Dr. Martin Seligman, the research focused on the role that positive psychology plays in the pursuit of happiness. This work also validates many statements made throughout this book that focus on how humans have the ability to determine their own life satisfaction.

## A Formula For Retirement Happiness

Scientists have had a very hard time predicting a person's level of happiness based on good or bad events he or she has experienced. Instead, a far better predictor is the beliefs and attitudes he or she maintains.
Our happiness is inextricably bound to the things in life that we value. Too often, however, we base our dreams of our future on activities or events that we would like to have happen without really understanding the real reason why those dreams would make us happy.

What is it that makes you happy? It stands to reason that if you could find a way to be happy each and every day for the rest of your life, you would lead a fulfilling life. We all strive to be happy, but do we all really know what is at the root of our happiness?

It's not the events that make us happy, or simply participating in activities. It's how they make us feel, the emotions they create inside us. And our emotions are stirred the most when we engage in activities directly linked to our core values.

*Happiness is that state of consciousness which proceeds from the achievement of one's values.*

— **Ayn Rand,** *author*

## Retirement Happiness Values: The Concept Of PERMA

PERMA is an acronym that describes five conditions that Dr. Seligman says will lead to "authentic happiness" at any age. Think of PERMA as the values that you should have to achieve a happy retirement.

**P**ositive Emotion: We know that optimists do better in retirement than pessimists, and that other-directed people do not fare as well in retirement as self-directed people. As you look at your retirement, are you excited or are you apprehensive? As someone once said, happiness is the way you live your life and not a desired state of being!

**E**ngagement: In retirement, it is easy to become disengaged from day-to-day life if your concept of "being involved" comes from your day-to-day work. People, who are more likely to go out with friends, undertake activities and remain mentally active feel more "alive" and enjoy more successful retirements. Take a look at Chapter 6 for more things to think about.

**R**elationships: Human beings are not meant to be on their own; we need other people who we can care for, have fun with and to expand our horizons. In retirement, the strength of our social network will be a major determinant in life satisfaction. However, relationships need to be positive to have the most impact on our overall retirement happiness. While men may have more relationships, women tend to have deeper relationships, and it is those nurturing, supporting relationships that matter. We have an in-depth discussion of relationships in Chapter 7.

**M**eaning: There is a big difference between fulfilling activities in retirement over time-filling. Maslow said that the peak of the needs pyramid is our need for self-actualization. Retirement is the time to look at the meaning of life and to focus on living a life of purpose. That is why we have adopted the concept of 'Second Life' rather than treating retirement as a 30-year-long weekend full of perpetual leisure! We address this issue more fully in Chapter 8.

**A**chievement: Self-image has a significant impact on our mental outlook, our relationships with others and our desire to continually feel good about ourselves. In retirement, it is easy to look in the mirror and to consider our physical age and the chronic physical conditions that we may have. It is also easy to reflect on our success at work that has disappeared now that we are retired. We need to win small and large victories, no matter how old we are.

## What Will You Do With This Information?

If you look at each area, what specific things can you do to engage yourself in activities that will lead to your retirement happiness?

| | Things I can do in my life | Specific plans today |
|---|---|---|
| **Positive Emotion**<br>*Optimism*<br>*Excitement*<br>*Taking charge* | | |
| **Engagement**<br>*Involvement*<br>*Fulfilling Activities*<br>*Community*<br>*Education* | | |
| **Relationships**<br>*Family*<br>*Social Network*<br>*Community* | | |
| **Meaning**<br>*Purpose*<br>*Goals*<br>*Values*<br>*Spirituality* | | |
| **Achievement**<br>*Big and small "wins"*<br>*Goal-setting*<br>*Bucket list*<br>*Work and education* | | |

### DID YOU KNOW?

• Reported levels of happiness were positively correlated and reported levels of sadness were negatively correlated with serotonin synthesis. (Perreau-Link, 2007, Journal of Psychiatry and Neuroscience)

• Happiness has nothing to do with aging. In fact, the later years can be the best time of your life. Many studies have shown that people get happier as they age. If you eat healthily, exercise, take care of your mind and stay connected with others, you can influence your happiness levels.

# CHAPTER 10
## The Ideal Retirement Attitude

### SOME THINGS TO CONSIDER:

• Why do some people seem to handle their transition into retirement easier than others?

• What role does stress play in retirement happiness?

• How can I develop a retirement personality that will make my retirement even better?

*This chapter focuses on the ideal attitudes to deal with the stresses and strains of retirement.* Scientists have identified those attributes in successful retirees. We will look at these and discuss how you can make your personality more "hardy."

### The Hardy Retirement Personality

Psychologists and behavioural scientists have done much work on the elements of personality that enable some of us to handle stress better than others. Your ability to handle stress without it affecting either your physical or emotional well-being is critical to navigating a successful transition into your Second Life.

Dr. Richard Johnson, a noted authority in retirement and adult development, feels that stress management is critical to a successful retirement. Dr. Johnson's work on the relationship between stress management and health suggests a major factor in healthy aging is our ability to keep stress at tolerable levels. In retirement, your ability to manage stress will influence not only your longevity, but also your day-to-day mental and physical health. We will examine the role that stress management plays in retirement planning later in this book when we discuss healthy aging.

One challenge we face with stress is that it can accumulate and progress without our being aware of it. It's not always a major stressful event that hits us, but the cumulative effect of smaller stressors that can cause us problems. In your Second Life, there may be a number of naturally stressful situations that could occur:

- Critical decisions regarding work, life purpose, etc.
- Health challenges faced by you and those closest to you
- Family and/or social relationships with demands that may cause you concern
- Lack of structure in your life after a lifetime of living with more clearly established guidelines
- Financial hiccups or challenges that cause you concern about your financial situation
- Lack of direction, boredom or inactivity

Researcher Suzanne Kobasa found that there is a direct correlation between the onset of stress-related illness and low scores in specific personality areas. As the result of Kobasa's research, and further research conducted at the University of Illinois, four elements of your personality—your "hardiness"—have emerged as the keys to handling stress.

A "hardy" personality consists of four key elements. Consider the affirmations below each element as a way to summarize each thought and embody them in your experience:

**1** **Control:** Hardy personalities believe that they have some control over events in their lives, their emotions, their well-being, etc. We referred to this early as "internal locus of control." While they know that they can't control everything in the world (life can often get in the way), they recognize that they can always control how they view events in their lives. "Hardies" tend to be planners and build strategies to achieve their goals. Their ability to handle stress comes in part because these individuals take responsibility for both successes and failures in life.

➡ I AM NOT POWERLESS OVER MY WORLD.

**2** **Commitment:** Hardy personalities are committed to themselves, their families, their community and their world. They strive for continual improvement, believing that they can use their abilities to control some things that would make their world better. Their belief spurs them to seek out new opportunities and challenges each day. These are individuals who are results-oriented and strive to achieve in their daily lives.

➡ MY LIFE, WORK, FAMILY AND FRIENDS ARE IMPORTANT. I CARE ABOUT WHAT I AM DOING.

**3** **Challenge:** Hardy personalities continually challenge their limits, pushing to learn new things, take new adventures and continue their personal growth. These individuals relish change and transition as an opportunity to "roll with the punches" and to test their personal mettle.

➡ CHANGE IS NORMAL AND NOT TO BE FEARED.
NEW SITUATIONS AND CHALLENGES ARE A CHANCE FOR GROWTH AND SUCCESS.

**4** **Connectedness:** Hardy personalities feel that they are part of a bigger picture. They feel connected to their sense of self, their families and friendships, their community, their world and their universe. In other words, they believe in something beyond themselves and feel that there is a sense of purpose that goes beyond simple existence.

➡ MY LIFE HAS MEANING AND I WILL STRIVE TO LIVE MY LIFE IN THE CONTEXT OF A LARGER WORLD/UNIVERSE.

## Relating PERMA Values To 'Hardy' Attitudes

As we noted earlier, the concept of PERMA is really an outline of the key values that you should have that have been tied to the concept of retirement happiness. Hardy personality traits help you stay healthy, both mentally and physically. A good way to look at the relationship between PERMA and the Hardy personality is:

| **VALUES** | | **HARDY ATTITUDES** |
|---|---|---|
| • Positive Emotion | | • Taking control |
| • Life engagement |  | • Commitment to living each day to its fullest |
| • Meaningful relationships | | • Continuing to challenge you |
| • Life meaning | | • Connecting with others |
| • Achievement | | |

## Increasing The 'Hardiness' Of Your Retirement Personality

If you engage in activities to increase the "hardiness" of your personality, you are also undertaking activities that will lead to retirement happiness. Here are some ways that you can do that and strengthen a hardy retirement personality:

• Hardy retirees make plans and take control. Individuals with "hardy" personalities are determined to target the elements that will contribute to making their Second Life fulfilling, and believe they have influence over things that will maintain their life satisfaction. For example, they expect and prepare for change and bounce back from challenges or emotional upsets faster.

• Hardy retirees care about their lives. These individuals choose to live active lives and stay socially connected.

• Hardy retirees feel that there is a reason to get out of bed in the morning. These individuals understand that if they lose their sense of purpose, they are sowing the seeds of an unhealthy and potentially shortened life. These individuals relish the activities they choose because they contribute directly to an overall sense of purpose, rather than just being meaningless activities they engage in to fill time. Whether you call this spirituality or self-efficacy, the fact is that a sense of meaning and purpose provides a life force that sustains them in retirement.

• Hardy retirees see retirement as a positive challenge that offers them the opportunity to try new things and to stretch and grow in new ways.

• A hardy personality can be learned. Suzanne Kobasa found in her research (1979) that it is possible to develop and increase your level of "hardiness." Kobasa feels that self-efficacy, or taking charge of your life and "making it happen" can be learned by people of all ages and can significantly change how people view the world.

Consider the people you know who have lost a job or a spouse or encountered a financial difficulty. There are those who buckle under the pressure, while others find some hidden strength to get through it. It remains a matter of attitude. If you really want to identify and control your stress in retirement, you can learn to do it!

*Here are some tips on improving the 'hardiness' of your retirement personality:*

- Accept that you have value to yourself and to others. Rather than shrinking away from others, seek out opportunities to interact and show them the real you.

- Accept the things you cannot change, and change the things you can. Retirement is your time to de-stress and to stop worrying about everything in your life.

- Be more independent (but not too much). You need to feel that you can depend on yourself, but remember that you need other people in your life for you to be really as good as you can be!

- Don't stop learning. Not only do you want to exercise your mind, but you can also use the power of learning to gain a sense of accomplishment in retirement. Plus, it makes you more interesting at parties!

- Become a goal setter. Small goals, big goals—it doesn't matter. Again, you get a sense of accomplishment but goal-setting helps you feel in control. Write lists, create plans and develop structure in your life.

- Be healthy. If you feel good about yourself, you will exude confidence around others. You will have more energy to do things and will more likely want to do new things.

- Value your friends and family. Relationships can be nurtured and supported. If you can develop new friendships and strengthen the ones you have, it will affect the hardiness of your personality.

# Exercise

## Assessing Your Hardy Personality

Below is a quick inventory of the "hardiness" of your retirement personality. Determine how much you are like each of the statements below using the following scale:

| 0 | 1 | 2 | 3 | 4 | 5 |
|---|---|---|---|---|---|
| Never | Seldom | Sometimes | Often | Usually | Always |

| | | |
|---|---|---|
| 1 | I have a written list of things that I would like to accomplish in my life that I update regularly as things are completed. | |
| 2 | I spend quiet time meditating and contemplating my life and my world. | |
| 3 | I wake up in the morning full of optimism and looking forward to starting my day. | |
| 4 | I have a clear picture of what the next phase of my life will look like. | |
| 5 | I try to learn as many new things as I can. | |
| 6 | I sleep well and am able to relax when I have free time. | |
| 7 | I believe that I have control over most things in my life. | |
| 8 | I look forward to the changes that happen in my life and view them as challenges. | |
| 9 | I feel that I have a purpose in life and I am clear on what that is. | |
| 10 | I am usually an optimistic person when it comes to how I view my future. | |
| 11 | I am adventuresome, continually pushing my limits to try new things. | |
| 12 | I would consider myself to be very goal-oriented. | |

## Total:

## Scoring the Hardy Personality Test

**0-24**   You may not feel in control of your world and may not spend a lot of time making plans. Your ability to handle stress is not as strong as you would like.

**25-36**   You do some planning, but probably wish you did more. You tend to be other-directed and not always in control of your life.

**37-48**   You are more self-directed and normally handle stress well. You tend to be goal-oriented, though you could be more focused on setting goals.

**49-60**   You are very goal-oriented and know the difference between being stressed and handling stress.

# Exercise

## Activities You Can Undertake To Increase Your 'Hardiness'

|  | Things I can do in my life | Specific plans today |
|---|---|---|
| **Taking Control** <br> *Making plans* <br> *Feeling like I have control* <br> *Taking initiative* |  |  |
| **Challenging myself** <br> *New activities or pursuits* <br> *Setting goals* <br> *Learning new things* <br> *Meeting new people* |  |  |
| **Commitment to life** <br> *Positive outlook* <br> *Doing new things* <br> *Getting out of the house* <br> *Meditating* |  |  |
| **Connecting to others** <br> Joining groups <br> Making new friends <br> Strengthening relationships <br> Seeking conversations |  |  |

## What Will You Do With This Information?

• We can learn a lot from successful people of retirement age about the Do's and Don'ts of building a happy Second Life.

• Attitude is more important than money when it comes to a happy retirement.

• Stress management is an important element of healthy aging; it directly influences your day-to-day mental and physical health, which directly impacts your quality of life.

• There are four distinct elements of a stress-resistant or hardy personality: control, commitment, challenge and connectedness.

• Having a "hardy personality" can be learned.

### DID YOU KNOW?

• A study of the Organization for Economic Co-operation and Development (OECD) nations concluded that verbal skills, communication and intelligence remain unchanged as a person ages.

• One of the best things you can do for your brain later in life, research shows, is learn a new language.

"Tom, come quick! Kinney in accounting has come up with a way to put a price on happiness!"

# CHAPTER 11
## Managing Change And Transition In Your Second Life

**SOME THINGS TO CONSIDER:**

• What changes may occur in your life in the future?

• Are you normally able to handle change without stress?

• Is change a good thing or a bad thing for you?

• What is your strategy to manage expected and unexpected changes in your life?

*The purpose of this chapter is to give you a strategy to manage changes that may occur in your future.* We will explore some of these changes and share some concepts that may help you to make a successful transition to your new reality.

"Let's eat out tonight."

Many people confuse the concepts of *change* and *transition*. In your Second Life, you will encounter several transitions that you can make happen or will happen anyway. You don't always have control over your transitions, at least not in the way that you want. But change is something that you do have control over because of the attitude you take.

Your Second Life will be one of change. That isn't an outlandish prediction. It just will.

If you consider some of the issues that we have discussed so far, it will be extremely important for you to have a strategy that will allow you to "roll with the punches." We talked earlier about negative stress and how it can affect your health. We also pointed out that this phase of our lives is one of many changes and that status quo is constantly being threatened.

### Here are some of the changes that can occur in your Second Life:

**Health:** Progression of chronic conditions, sudden health events, hormonal issues such as menopause and andropause (male menopause), mental or physical decline or incapacity, caregiving and bereavement

**Relationships:** Loss of friends or family, physical or mental incapacity (yours or theirs), bereavement, conflict, caregiving, death of a pet

**Work:** Decline in physical or mental capacity, forced retirement, business failure or change, voluntary retirement

**Leisure:** Physical or mental incapacity or challenge, loss of leisure partners, financial challenge

**Home:** Downsizing, long-term care, moving in with family, location and proximity to friends and family (in fact, moving to a new location as part of your "ideal" retirement can be one of the most stressful retirement experiences)

**Financial:** Financial setback, investment reversal, overspending, unexpected financial demand, caregiving expenses and bereavement

Each one of these will present a challenge to you if they result in the end of the way that you are currently living part of your life. How you respond will affect your overall health and future happiness.

## The Phases Of Retirement

Traditional retirement is a good example of the changes that occur over a period of time. There have been many explanations of the phases of retirement: some focus on financial issues, some on health or leisure issues.

Since this book focuses on the psychology of retirement, let's look at the changes that can occur as you age in retirement. The timelines are simply suggestions. Each person will have a different experience, but here are some rough guidelines.

## Retirement Stages

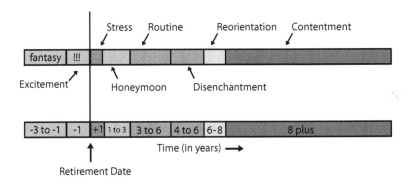

**Fantasy Stage:** In those last years of work prior to retirement, the concept of retirement lifestyle is more fiction than fact (normally from one to three years before the expected retirement date). It is the time to dream about all of the things you want to do in this phase of life. Dreams of trips to be taken or toys to be bought mark the fantasy stage. This is a good time to focus on specific plans rather than dreaming.

**Excitement Stage:** In the last year prior to retirement, pre-retirees focus on the retirement date in the same way as we would the start of a holiday or anticipation of a special event. You should focus on finalizing plans and strategies for the future. The retirement date becomes the start date for the next phase of life rather than the end date of a work career.

**Stress Stage:** Reality sets in. Now that retirement has started, it is common for new retirees in the first year to focus on fears and concerns about this new life. Retirement is an adjustment and your focus will likely be on making that adjustment to day-to-day life.

**Honeymoon:** From one to three years after retirement, retirees try to do all of the things that they had dreamt of in the fantasy stage. This is the perpetual long weekend. This is also the time when retirees tend to spend excessively as they adjust to a new lifestyle.

**Routine:** At some point, at roughly the three-year point, you will likely move into the routine phase. This is after the initial glow wears off and the fact that retirement is a day-to-day way of living becomes apparent. This period of life will last until a health challenge gets in the way and forces you to make an adjustment.

**Disenchantment:** Commonly, this will occur somewhere between four to six years after retirement. However, it can occur at any time. Most often, the disenchantment stage is marked by recognition of your mortality. This is the stage where depression is common as you are forced to adjust to a new lifestyle because of health issues, or life alone due to bereavement. This is also the stage where the retiree's spirit is challenged.

**Reorientation:** The successful retiree will make an adjustment to his or her new reality.

**Contentment:** Finally, the last stage is contentment as the retiree has created a new life and is adjusting to it. Some never do and are stuck in the disenchantment stage.

## Handling Change And Transition

*Unless transition occurs, change will not.*
— **William Bridges,** *author*

Our discussion above focuses on changes that can occur that will cause you to take a fresh look at your life and adjust to the change. A new reality occurs as you adjust to a life that has changed, probably forever. The challenge is to allow the change to occur so that you can move on rather than being stuck in the past and not able to move forward.

Jack, age 61, was formerly a pilot and flew all over the world in his job. At parties, he would be a centre of attention as people quizzed him about places he had been and things they had always wondered about regarding airplanes and his life. He looked forward to many more years of flying, thankful that the rules allowed him to continue past age 65. Then, an unexpected health problem interrupted his job and prevented him from flying. As a result, Jack was forced to retire.

Since his retirement, Jack has been miserable. Everything about what he thought he was and the life that he loved was now changed. Each day since, he spends time reminiscing about the past and longing to fly jets again. He has not yet made the transition into a new life.

## Bridges' Transition Model

In his ground-breaking work *Transitions: Making Sense of Life's Changes*, author William Bridges created a simple model of how we move through the stages of our lives and process change. His model is a great explanation of how important the planning process is in moving us from one life stage to another and the foundation of this chapter.

Bridges' change model is simple, but its implication on retirement planning is profound:

First, there is an ending of the life that you had. For example, Jack can no longer fly. That's done.  Bridges calls this "the end of the old order." If you think about the changes that we looked at above, there are things in your retirement life that will change. It could be a simple change, such as your knee gives out and you can no longer play tennis; or a change could be catastrophic, such as the death of a spouse.

From this event, you move to the "neutral zone." The neutral zone is that time that allows us to think about the future, the things we want to accomplish and the plans that we need to make. When someone moves from work to their new retirement life, there can be feelings of fear, anxiety, emptiness, confusion or disenchantment, particularly if the new retiree had looked at this new life as a prolonged holiday rather than a life change.

## Chaos Or Creativity?

The neutral zone can be the catalyst for one of two things: chaos, or creativity. Chaos comes from not being able to handle the change or to move away from a reality that no longer exists. Creativity, on the other hand, is the opportunity to make something out of a new life that you have now been forced into.

Bridges states, "The importance of the neutral zone is not the length of time that one stays in this phase of life but that the person uses whatever time they have productively." This is the impetus, therefore, to take a look at all aspects of retirement and to prepare to move forward from the "old" life.

In fact, for a retiree whose identity is bound to his previous career, the neutral zone is the time that he can take to move forward and put the past behind. It is also helpful in coping with bereavement, loss of a parent or a health challenge.

**The keys to managing the neutral zone for prospective retirees are:**

> • Don't wait until retirement until you start thinking about your plans for the future.
> • "Practise" retirement while you are still working to identify potential planning areas.
> • Look at all areas of your life and assess the impact of the retirement transition.
> • Don't limit retirement planning to a financial plan. The financial plan comes after the life plan.

William Bridges writes: "*It is a time between the old life and the new. It can be a particularly rich time for such insight. It can be a time of truly 'seeing' (retirement) life for what it is.*"

## Planning For The Expected And Unexpected

Can you plan for life's changes ahead of time? The answer is not a simple one; yes, you can plan for things that *may* happen as well as for those things that *will* happen.

You just don't know when. Our experience is that many people wear rose-coloured glasses when it comes to planning for retirement, and this includes financial advisors as well as their clients.

As one advisor told us, "I don't like to focus my clients on too many negative things because I want them to enjoy their visit with me." We also find that people think retirement planning is just creating a bucket list of wonderful things to do because, after all, who wants to be all "doom and gloom"?

While this "head in the sand" approach is understandable, it is not doing you any favours. So, here is a strategy that you can use to discuss all of the possible things that can go wrong with your plan while still leaving time for your "bucket list of dreams."

## The 'Fire Drill'

As you are making your retirement plans, take a set length of time (15 to 30 minutes should work) and talk about all of the possible things that might occur in the future and what your plans should be if they happen. Then, when the time is done, move on to the good things about retirement planning and put your fire drill plans back on the shelf until next time.

## Financial Implications Of Life Changes

Life changes can result in financial changes that may affect your life even further. You should consider the possible impact of these as you make your plans (or have your fire drill).

| Life Transition Event | Some Possible Financial Implications | |
|---|---|---|
| Death of a spouse | • Wills, probate, etc.<br>• Insurance policies<br>• Employment-related issues<br>• Inheritance<br>• Burial and final expenses | • Financial planning for remaining spouse<br>• Disposal of assets<br>• Loss of income<br>• Change in financial situation |
| Critical Illness | • Income replacement<br>• Insurance issues<br>• Asset management | • Health-care costs<br>• Change in work situation |
| Divorce | • Inventory of assets<br>• Disposal of assets<br>• Managing settlements | • Day-to-day financial management concerns<br>• Tax implications<br>• Income changes |
| Retirement | • Income changes<br>• Expense changes<br>• Standard of living changes | • Insurance changes<br>• Housing changes |
| Caregiving | • Change in work and income situation<br>• Added expenses for care | • Change in residence<br>• Powers of attorney |
| Moving | • Cost of move<br>• Increased expenses at new place<br>• Construction or repair costs | |

# Exercise

## Your Retirement Changes

While we can't anticipate exactly when a change will occur, we should consider the probability in terms of changes that could occur in the next year, the next five years and beyond five years.

Take a look at each change and try to forecast when it might occur for either you or your spouse or partner. Then, check the right-hand column if you have talked about what would happen should this occur.

| Life Change | Within the next year? | Within the next five years? | Five years and beyond? | Plan in place? |
|---|---|---|---|---|
| **Health** | | | | |
| Chronic conditions | | | | |
| Sudden health condition (heart attack, stroke, etc.) | | | | |
| Mental or physical decline | | | | |
| Incapacity | | | | |
| Caregiving | | | | |
| **Relationships** | | | | |
| Loss of friends | | | | |
| Loss of companion | | | | |
| Loss of pet | | | | |
| Caregiving | | | | |
| Family conflict | | | | |
| Loss of parents | | | | |
| **Work** | | | | |
| Mental or physical incapacity | | | | |
| Forced retirement | | | | |
| Change in business | | | | |
| Voluntary retirement | | | | |
| **Leisure** | | | | |
| Physical or mental incapacity or decline | | | | |
| Loss of companion | | | | |
| Financial challenge | | | | |

| Life Change | Within the next year? | Within the next five years? | Five years and beyond? | Plan in place? |
|---|---|---|---|---|
| **Home** | | | | |
| Downsizing | | | | |
| Assisted care | | | | |
| Moving to new location | | | | |
| Moving in with family | | | | |
| **Financial** | | | | |
| Retirement | | | | |
| Inheritance | | | | |
| Helping children or grandchildren | | | | |
| Sale of home or business | | | | |

## What Will You Do With This Information?

There is an old saying: Forewarned is forearmed. Simply put, the more you recognize the issues that could happen, the more you are prepared to withstand them and then make any transition to your new reality.

Are there things that you can do to reduce the likelihood of any of these events being a negative or causing you undue distress?

# PART 4

*HEALTHY AGING IN YOUR SECOND LIFE*

# CHAPTER 12
## Healthy Aging

## SOME THINGS TO CONSIDER:

• What do you know about the physical aspects of aging?

• How would you characterize your overall physical health today?

• How active would you like to be in your Second Life?

• Are you doing positive things today that may influence your longevity and quality of life in the future?

• What negative habits do you have that may threaten your healthy aging?

In this chapter, we will address the issue of healthy aging and its importance in retirement. Remember, though, that this discussion has to involve both physical and mental health. Since so much of this book focuses on healthy mental aging, we are using this chapter to address the physical issues.

Remember the movie About Schmidt with Jack Nicholson? In the movie, Jack's character was a 65-year-old insurance actuary who didn't want to retire but was forced to. His retirement plan with his wife was to buy a big motorhome and tour America. I remember how poignant the scene was when they first had breakfast in their RV while it was still sitting in the driveway.

Within a month of his retirement, and before they had a chance to begin to live their retirement dreams, Schmidt's wife died suddenly. As I watched, I was thinking about how often health challenges get in the way of the great plans people have for retirement. While there are some health challenges that we can't prevent, there are so many things that we can do to maximize our chances for optimum health in our Second Lives.

## What Is Healthy Aging?

Health issues will certainly impact our retirement years. Remember the old cliché "Age doesn't matter unless you are cheese"? Even if we maintain good health as we age, we may notice a few more aches and pains and find some things just don't work as well as they used to.

It seems that people often don't recognize just how important good health is for a successful retirement. In fact, surveys of our retirement workshop participants indicate that many pre-retirees believe that "having enough money" is going to be more important to their future success and life enjoyment than good health.

*Health is not simply the absence of sickness.*

— **Hannah Green**

## Getting In The Way Of 'Best Laid Plans'

There is little doubt that many aging boomers are concerned about sustaining their feelings of youth, or at least looking young, in retirement. Both men and women continue to search for the fountain of youth by colouring their hair, getting Botox injections, trying out new forms of non-invasive facelifts and buying an endless number of vitamins and supplements.

Ironically, this same group of boomers seems to be hiding their heads in the sand regarding health-related issues that truly could impact their well-being as they age.

In one example, a study conducted in the U.S. by Roper found that while 89% of U.S. boomers understood that having high blood pressure and high cholesterol greatly increases the risk of heart attack or stroke, a majority was unaware of what their own levels were. In another example, author and internist Dr. Henry Lodge estimated that "70% of premature death and aging is lifestyle-related" and entirely preventable.

## Let's Start With The Bad News First...

We might as well get it out of the way so that we can focus on creating a positive plan for the future. We are not as healthy as the pre-war generation.

Many boomers smugly believe that their awareness of health issues makes them healthier than older siblings or parents. It seems, however, that our behaviour isn't keeping pace with our knowledge. Earlier, we quoted Gail Sheehy who suggested that 50 is now yesterday's 40. Can we say from a physical standpoint that 65 is really yesterday's 50? Maybe not!

Here is how the boomer population stacks up against a previous generation of Americans:

### The Current State of American boomers' Health

- 61% have insufficient physical activity
- 38% are obese and 39% overweight
- 17% smoke
- 34% have a life-time risk of harm from alcohol (disease or injury)
- 21% have high blood pressure
- 47% have high cholesterol
- 57% have vitamin D deficiency

Many boomers feel that they have better health than their parents at this age of life. However, the numbers suggest that the pursuit of lifestyle may have had some detrimental effect on overall health as this cohort enters retirement.

We could go on, but you get the picture. There are some things that will happen to you in retirement that are part of the natural aging process—the result of cells breaking down. Gerontologists call this senescence. Senescence happens at a different rate for each of us; but it will ultimately happen to all of us. The good news? There are many things we can do to extend our longevity and to improve the quality of life as we age.

## It Probably Isn't Too Late

Jack was a 62-year-old executive in a manufacturing firm. Like many Americans, he had spent years working long hours, eating poorly and developing a lot of habits that left him in less than desirable physical health.

"I had developed my retirement plans and was ready to walk away from the job," he told us. "One of the things I knew I needed to address was how I felt. I knew that I lacked the energy I needed to really enjoy life. I was concerned that my retirement wouldn't last very long the way I was going."

In consultation with his doctor, Jack looked to change a lot of the things that were holding him back. A change in his eating patterns combined with a regular walking routine helped him to drop 40 pounds over six months. He stopped smoking entirely and added vitamin supplements to his daily regimen. His energy returned and he progressed toward a healthy lifestyle that would support him through his retirement years.

Fortunately for Jack, research tells us that our bodies have an amazing ability to rebound if we make even small changes in how we treat ourselves.

"At any time you decide to improve your behaviour and make lifestyle changes, they make a difference from that point on," says Dr. Jeffrey Koplan, a former director of the Centers for Disease Control and Prevention (CDC) in Atlanta. "Maybe not right away, but it's like slamming on the brakes. You do need a certain skid distance."

As Dr. Thomas Perls and Margery Silver state in Living to 100, "The goal is not to make everyone a super being who can swim the English Channel at 85. Rather, we want to help people gain more years of excellent health so they can do the things they enjoy or explore new things for the first time."

### Consider these facts:

• Women who add eight ounces of fish per week to their diet decrease their risk of stroke by half, according to the Journal of the American Medical Association.

• Eating more fruits and vegetables changes our body's sensitivity to insulin within just two weeks, decreasing the likelihood of diabetes immediately. Vitamin C can also lower stroke risk.

• Once you stop smoking, the carbon monoxide in your system declines right away. Within just five years, you have decreased your likelihood of having a smoking-related heart attack to the same level as someone who had never smoked.

• A 40-year-old woman who has led a sedentary lifestyle and then starts a four-day-a-week half-hour walking routine, can very quickly decrease her risk of a heart attack to the same level as someone else who has exercised all her life.

## Mental And Physical Health

We have the ability to kill ourselves physically by killing ourselves mentally. It is our values that drive our actions. Our mental health will go a long way toward driving our physical health; if we decide that a key to successful aging will be feeling well, our minds can make that happen. On the other hand, if "being healthy" is not a value that we hold, then we are less likely to make fitness part of our daily routine.

# What Will You Do With This Information?

## Start to Create a Healthy Retirement Today

Healthy aging is crucial for enjoying your retirement and should be a vital part of your retirement plan. However, this is one area of your plan you don't want to put off until you actually retire. Lifestyle habits that will affect your future health must be addressed now. Three keys to creating a healthy lifestyle in retirement are exercise, diet, and healthy lifestyle habits. It is estimated that by incorporating all three of these factors, disability can be delayed by as much as 10 years.

Exercise has many benefits throughout our lives. As we age exercise becomes more important rather than less important. Some people think that older people need to rest. The truth is the older we get, the more we need to get up and move around!

## Exercising for Retirement

Many of us groan when we hear the word exercise. Yet exercise can and should be fun. If you do activities you enjoy, you are much more likely to keep doing them. This is a great time for creativity. Think back to what you liked to do when you were a child and look for clues to what you would enjoy doing today. If you loved to ride your bike as a child, it is very possible that you would still enjoy that today. Remember, you are in this for the long haul so you want to find exercise that brings you pleasure, not that you have to endure.

By the way, you are no longer 21 years old. Make sure that your exercise program is appropriate for your physical health and current level of fitness!

**"I'm impressed, 100 skips in 60 seconds - but you still have to retire now that you have reached retirement age."**

The best type of exercise program is one that incorporates aerobic, strength training, and stretching. Aerobic exercise is important because by age 65 aerobic capacity has typically decreased by 30% to 40%. This decline is significantly less in people who exercise. Aerobic exercise has many benefits, including lowering blood pressure, improving our cholesterol and triglyceride levels, and burning fat—a benefit many of us would like!

Strength training is also very important as we age. Without regular exercise, we lose muscle mass and gain body fat as we age. Strength training can prevent and even reverse this process. It also increases our metabolism so we burn more calories, even when we are resting! And strength training is particularly important as we age because it reduces the risk of falls, increases the density of our bones and helps strengthen our tendons and joints right along with our muscles.

You can still do strength training even if you aren't someone who wants to go lift weights at the gym. Instead try stretch bands, "flexi balls," and strengthening videos you can use at home. There is even a Weight Training for Dummies book that can help!

Stretching is the third type of exercise we all need to do. Stretching increases our flexibility and keeps us limber for day-to-day activities we need to perform. Without doing stretching exercises, people become less flexible as they age. This may not seem like a big issue now, but it may be in the future if you have trouble manoeuvring in and out of your car or reaching your toes to cut your toenails! Try yoga, Pilates or just stretching out on your bedroom floor with some simple stretching exercises.

Maintaining a balanced diet and making good lifestyle choices are also important factors in creating a healthy retirement. Visit your health care professionals on a regular basis and get appropriate testing and monitoring for weight, blood pressure, cholesterol, and blood sugar. In addition you should ask your doctor about other tests you might need at various ages to ensure good health.

## A Stitch In Time...

In our workshops, participants building their retirement transition plans often say that they intend to be active at 70 or 80 years old. They see themselves walking along the ocean or hiking in the Appalachians and being the poster child for the fit senior American!

While that is a noble goal, remember that it is difficult to start from scratch if you were not physically active when you were younger. If an active lifestyle in retirement is truly your goal, it is a good idea to start now to incorporate more exercise and stretching into your routine in your 40s, 50s and 60s.

## Healthy Lifestyle And Your Money

When you think about a healthy lifestyle, you also want to consider the length of time that your money may have to last until you finally pass away. While that is a positive outcome of being healthy and a worthy goal, there is the opposite potential. Medical science and good exercise may have found answers to how you can protect yourself from dying quickly. However, as you get older and frailer, you and your partner may require costly critical care that you may not be able to afford.

Ask yourself who will look after you if you become infirm? If you are in the position today to take a close look at disability or critical care insurance, you may want to discuss this option with your financial advisor.

Remember that you will likely be in retirement for a long time, particularly if you are healthy, and you will want to continue with an active lifestyle for as long as possible. That can cause some financial pressure if you haven't planned to have your money last as long as you do! Your financial advisor can help you build a long-term investment strategy that doesn't have to end when you reach 71.

Finally, we never know how long our good health will last or when our time will be up. Always ensure that your estate plan, including your will, is up-to-date and that you have discussed everything with your partner.

## *A Dozen Strategies For Healthy Eating And Controlling Weight In Retirement:*

1. Research shows that weight control is a matter of calories in versus calories out. In other words, balance your caloric intake with your level of activity or energy expenditure in order to maintain a healthy weight as you age.

2. Avoid the "magic bullet" or a quick fix to losing or maintaining a healthy weight. Positive nutritional habits that you can manage and maintain over time are the key to success.

3. Make your health and well-being a priority. Do not put your own needs on hold for anybody else. Discover your own motivation for getting on track. Maybe it's your doctor's advice, maybe it's realizing you're out of breath doing a simple activity, or maybe it's a desire to be more active with your grandchildren.

4. Write down what you eat. This will help you to discover what is really going on and help you to make wiser choices.

5. Weigh yourself regularly. Your weight will naturally fluctuate by a couple of pounds either way, so don't obsess over the number. Instead, look for trends and adjust your efforts accordingly.

6. Set small goals. Losing just 10% of your body weight (20 pounds for someone who weighs 200 pounds) is very beneficial. Once you achieve a small goal, then try for more.

7. Plan ahead. Make an eating plan that includes 5-9 servings of fruits and vegetables and 2-3 servings of low-fat dairy products daily. These foods are filling and are low in calories. Include protein, of course, and even some higher-calorie favourites, but keep the portions small and savour every bite.

8. Don't skip meals. Eat healthy snacks between meals—every four to five hours. Discover those reasonable snacks that you truly enjoy so you don't feel deprived!

9. Set reasonable limits on eating meals out, especially fast food. People tend to eat more when they eat out, and they give up control of food preparation. If you do eat out, check out the menu ahead online for healthy options and be mindful of portions. Consider splitting your meal with your restaurant companion or taking half of your entrée home with you.

10. Avoid using food as your major coping mechanism. Look for alternative ways to reward yourself, divert your mind, handle stress, relax and give yourself comfort.

11. Develop and expand your support system and social activities beyond food. Spend time with people who share your interest in maintaining a healthy lifestyle. And as we've mentioned above, stay active and exercise—both major ingredients in maintaining a healthy weight.

12. Eat mindfully. People tend to eat more—roughly 300 calories more—than they need to each day. Be aware of what you eat during the day. An extra 100 calories a day can add up to 10 more pounds in just a year's time.

*(Adapted from The Duke Diet and Fitness Center, Durham, N.C., and the National Weight Control Registry, developed by Rena Wing, PhD, at Brown University, University of Pittsburgh, and James Hill, PhD, at the University of Colorado.)*

One of the best things you can do to improve your health is to quit smoking. You may hear people say it is too late to quit, that they have already done too much damage to their bodies. The truth is that as long as you are still breathing, it is not too late to quit! Life Insurance companies begin to reduce insurance rates one year after someone has stopped smoking. They do this because the health benefits are so dramatic. If you smoke, talk to your doctor about effective methods for quitting smoking. This is one area where the expression "If first you don't succeed, try, try again" absolutely applies.

## Seven Tips for a Healthier Retirement:

**Note:** *You should check with your MD before starting any diet or exercise program.*

1. Strive to incorporate exercise into your daily routine.

2. Balance your exercise program with endurance, strength training and stretching.

3. Evaluate your diet and determine small changes you can make over time, such as adding more fruits and vegetables.

4. Add a relaxation technique, such as meditation, to your daily routine.

5. Know your numbers: be aware of your blood pressure and cholesterol, and monitor them at regular intervals.

6. Make important lifestyle changes such as stopping smoking.

7. Lighten up and have fun.

# Exercise

## How Would You Rate Your Health Today?

As you think about your plans for your Second Life, step back for a moment and do a quick assessment of where you think your physical health is today.

| Health Habit Questions | YES | | YES |
|---|---|---|---|
| 1. I am a non-smoker. | 4 | 10. The amount of sugar or honey that I add to my food is less than one teaspoon per day. | 3 |
| 2. I eat less than two processed meat portions per week (bacon, bologna, etc.). | 2 | 11. I do stretching and limbering exercises every day. | 4 |
| 3. I eat a high-fibre diet, one that includes vegetables, roughage whole grains, etc. | 2 | 12. I am within 10 pounds of my ideal weight for my height and frame. | 4 |
| 4. I avoid butter, creams and other fats, including fried foods | 2 | 13. I have an easy time handling life's transitions and view them as challenges. | 2 |
| 5. I eat meat or other high-fat, high- cholesterol foods no more than once a day. | 2 | 14. I find time every day to do some of the things that I love to do. | 2 |
| | | 15. On the whole, my relationships bring me pleasure rather than stress. | 2 |
| 6. I don't drink more than two drinks of alcohol per day (a man), or one drink of alcohol per day (a woman) (12 oz. of beer or 5 oz. of wine per drink). | 3 | 16. I get at least six hours sleep every night. | 4 |
| | | 17. I limit the amount of caffeine that I drink to no more than two cups coffee per day. | 4 |
| 7. At least once a day, I perform a relaxation technique such as meditation or quiet contemplation. | 2 | 18. I protect myself from the sun as much as possible. | 3 |
| | | 19. I feel in control of my life most of the time. | 2 |
| 8. I drink at least four glasses of water per day. | 3 | 20. I do at least 20 minutes of exercise, at least four times a week. | 4 |
| 9. I eat candy, potato chips or other types of processed food less than twice a week | 2 | **Your Total:** | |

*If you scored:*

• More than 40 points, your score indicates a life style that encourages good health practices

• 33-39 points, you have incorporated a significant number of good health practices, and might find ways to add even more.

• Less than 33 points, you might want to start adding more good health practices to your lifestyle.

*If I'd known I was going to live so long, I'd have taken better care of myself.*
— **Eubie Blake,** *ragtime and jazz pianist (1887-1983)*

**A great website to look at on life expectancy!**
**www.livingto100.com**

**What's your life expectancy?** Life expectancy can often be related to family health history and your own lifestyle choices. Many people consider themselves healthy, but when asked a series of relevant questions, may revise their thinking. It will take you 10 minutes to answer the questions on this life-expectancy calculator to get an indication of how long you will live!

## DID YOU KNOW?

• The World Health Organization states, "Health is a state of complete physical, mental and social well-being and not merely the absence of disease or infirmity."

• Researchers Evans and Rosenberg (1991) found that "you do have a second chance to right the wrongs you have committed against your body. The markers of biological aging cannot only be altered, but, in the case of specific physiological functions, they can actually be reversed."

• Energy levels in the body don't depend on age—they depend on your attitude and are influenced by the quality of your life. Meditation, restful sleep, and exercise are the best ways to experience a joyful and energetic body.

• Women who drink only wine and no other type of alcoholic beverages are 70% less apt to develop dementia, according to a recent U.S study.

# CHAPTER 13
## The Role That Stress Plays As You Age

**SOME THINGS TO CONSIDER:**

• What situations do you face daily that upset you?

• As you think about this next phase of life, do you have a lot of worries?

• Are you excited about the future or apprehensive?

• Is retirement the "end" for you or just the beginning?

Greg, a 58-year-old irrigation specialist in the southern U.S., expects to retire in the next couple of years. Although he is self-employed, he has decided that he dislikes the work that he has done for the past 40 years and is ready for a rest. "I am so tired of waking up at 4 a.m. every day to go to work," he told us. "What I really want is to go to my cabin and fish every day."

Greg's wife Devona has seen her husband's increasing unhappiness for many years. She worries that he keeps everything inside and that he doesn't have many close friends. He can be irritated by small things and never seems to smile. She is concerned that he doesn't have any plans for retirement other than to go further into his funk.

## Positive And Negative Stress

The three major causes of death among American (as well as Canadian, Australian and British) seniors are stress-related diseases: lung cancer, cardiovascular and strokes. There is a direct link between our ability to handle stress as we age and our longevity.

## Not All Stress Is Equal

*That which does not kill us makes us stronger.*
— **Frederich Nietzsche,** *philosopher*

The state of negative stress that causes physical and emotional pain is known as *distress*. While we can never really get rid of distress, we can have control over how we respond to it. In fact, researchers have coined the term *Eustress* to describe positive stress or how some people create a reaction to negative stress that is both psychologically and physiologically positive.

The phrase "turning lemons into lemonade" describes Eustress. If you frame your challenges in terms of how you can make something out of them, you will go a long way toward healthy aging in your Second Life.

There can be many major stressors in this phase of life that may change the way you feel and the extent to which you are in distress. In 1967, Thomas Holmes and Richard Rahes developed their famous stress test that assigned a negative value to 43 different adult life events. They called these "life change units," and ranked them from 100 (high) to 0 (low) on their effects on people's lives. They also found a direct correlation between high levels of stress as measured in their test and incidence of illness.

*Consider these possible events in retirement and the life change units associated with them:*

• Death of a spouse (100)
• Divorce (73)
• Marital separation (65)
• Death of a close family member (63)
• Personal illness (53)

- Marriage (50)
- Marital reconciliation (45)
- Retirement (45)
- Death of a close friend (37)
- Child leaving home (35)
- Change in living conditions (25)

*The authors of the study tied the presence of stressful events to the risk of illness:*

- Score of 300+: At risk of illness.
- Score of 150-299: Risk of illness is moderate (reduced by 30% from the above risk).
- Score <150: Only have a slight risk of illness.

## Our System's Response To Stress

Scientific research shows that stress has a direct impact on your retirement happiness and healthy aging.

If your ability to manage or reframe stress is key to your retirement health, it makes sense to look at how you respond to both positive and negative stress and what you can do about it. You can then consider changes in your outlook and the way that you frame your life in order to create a more hardy retirement personality.

*When you are under negative or distress, your body will produce two influential hormones:*

**Cortisol,** produced in the adrenal glands, fights stress by suppressing the immune system, increasing blood sugar and decreasing bone formation.

**Norepinephrine** is a stress hormone, responsible for our fight-or-flight response. It increases the heart rate and blood pressure, releasing glucose, increasing awareness and increasing blood flow to skeletal muscles and away from internal organs.

*When you create Eustress to manage negativity and distress, your endocrine system will create two other hormones:*

**Serotonin** is called the satisfaction or happiness hormone. It is produced when you are experiencing pleasure, relaxation, achievement and a sense of peace. It is closest in nature to norepinephrine and can actually mask the negative effects!

**Dopamine** is the "alertness" hormone, essential to effective decision-making, motivation and clarity. It can override cortisol and cause you to take charge of your situation and find ways to make it better.

## Let The Positive Outweigh The Negative

It would make sense to create more dopamine and serotonin to counteract the effects of norepinephrine and cortisol. Think of it as a simple formula: the positive things that you do will outweigh the negative stress that you feel. In retirement, that means:

• Feeling that you are in control. That is why you have plans, stick to a structure and empower your mind to reframe negatives into positives;

• Being committed to living each day to its fullest. That means finding the good things about each day and being positive about the future;

• Continuing to look for opportunities for achievement in your life, both big and small;

• Connecting to people.

In your Second Life, you want to do more things that will create positive responses to negative situations. As we discussed earlier, this is a direct result of the positive attitude that you have and your desire to take control of your own reality. For review, revisit Chapter 9 on the hardy personality and Chapter 8 on the relationship between PERMA and retirement happiness.

Also, consider the information that we have provided you on the role of work (Chapter 2) and balanced or 'flow' leisure later in Chapter 22.

# Exercise

## How do you handle stress in your life?

As you consider the things that happen to you over the course of a day, how able are you to "roll with the punches" and handle negative stress? Here are some common stressors in our busy lives. Tick the ones that apply to how you live or view your life:

### Do you...

☐ Neglect your health

☐ Get easily upset at other people

☐ Fail to see the humour in situations that others find funny

☐ Dislike change

☐ Act rudely

☐ Feel that you are losing your zest for life

☐ Seldom take time to relax during the day

☐ Look to others to make things happen

☐ Resent structure, deadlines and expectations

☐ Have difficulty making decisions

☐ Feel disorganized

☐ Feel uncomfortable around people who disagree with your views

☐ Keep your emotions inside

☐ Avoid exercise

☐ Feel that you are addicted to things that could be bad for you

☐ Lack supporting relationships

☐ Self-medicate with pills, drugs or alcohol

☐ Get too little rest

☐ Like to talk about other people or gossip

☐ Ignore stress symptoms

☐ Feel uncomfortable in the relationships that you are in

☐ Refuse to take advice when doing something

☐ Refrain from making plans

☐ Get stuck on things that happened in the past

☐ Make a big deal out of everything

**Scoring this exercise:**
If you ticked:

**0-7:** You are likely a "low-stress" person. It appears that you have things under control in your life and that you have developed some good strategies to handle the things that could be stressful each day.

**8-13:** Generally you handle stress well. However, there are situations where you would be better off taking a deep breath before reacting. As you plan for retirement, you should find ways to strength your hardy personality. (See chapter 9.)

**13-19:** Your personal thermometer is rising and there could be danger ahead in your retirement, based on how you react to situations. Be aware of the dangers ahead if you continue to react to your situations in the way you do.

**More than 20:** Yikes! As you look at your attitudes toward life, your relationships with others and your approach to healthy aging, you must find ways to reframe the stressors and your reactions to them. You may miss many opportunities to get the most of your Second Life by focusing on negative things.

## What Will You Do With This Information?

### DID YOU KNOW?

• Research conducted at the University of Wisconsin found that a feeling of well-being and life purpose was higher in those people who had lower levels of cortisol during the day. (Lindfors and Lundbeck, 2002; Ryff, Singer, 2004)

• Our minds can produce serotonin to influence positive moods, or use positive moods to produce serotonin. (Perreau-Link et al., Journal of Psychiatry and Neuroscience, 2007)

• Low dopamine levels can cause depression, a loss of satisfaction, addictions, cravings, compulsions, low sex drive and an inability to focus.

# CHAPTER 14
## The Natural Course Of Aging

### SOME THINGS TO CONSIDER:
• Do you find yourself thinking "I am too old" to do something?

• How do you really feel about "getting older"?

• Do you try to look younger or feel young?

### 'How Old Would You Be…'

American baseball pitcher Satchel Paige played professional baseball until he was 60. He was considered to be a physical marvel and he had a unique answer to the question, "How old are you?"

"How old would you be…if you didn't know how old you are?"

Paige's philosophy was that you are "only as old as you feel".

### Handling The Aging Process

Everyone has a different way of handling the aging process psychologically. Positive aging is a term used to describe how to successfully adapt to "getting older," including feeling 'fit' both physically and mentally. There is a direct correlation between positive aging and longevity: studies suggest that those who take an optimistic view of the future and their mental and physical health will live an average of 7.5 years longer than those who are less positive. (Levy, Slade and Kunkle et al., Journal of Personality and Social Psychology, 2002, is just one of many studies that have drawn this link.)

The markers of healthy aging and their positive effect on your Second Life have been discussed in earlier chapters Chapters 11 and 12. as well as its positive impact on your Second Life. Positive aging refers to how you feel about getting older and your ability to maintain your positive outlook through both happy and trying times.

Your personality contributes a considerable amount to how you view your age. The more 'hardy' "hardy" your personality and the more that PERMA values are a part of your life, the more positive you will be about aging.

## *There are four ways that retirees view aging:*

### Age Irrelevance
Age is just a number and doesn't have a significant impact on your psyche. You may remember how old you are on your birthday but really don't care beyond that. You are likely more of an in-the-moment person and don't think or care much about your future.

### Age Affirmation
Aging is a positive experience and you relish who you are at any age. In fact, you often will be excited about getting older and the opportunities that age can bring to you. You appreciate the fabric of life and understand its "ages and stages." You also likely have a positive attitude about life and live more in the moment.

### Age Denial
Aging is a negative in your life and you refuse to believe that you are the age you are. That's not all bad, except you wish that you were a lot younger! You may undergo surgery, wear youthful clothing, heavy makeup or other aids in the search for eternal youth. Again, this is not necessarily bad, except that you can actually prolong your life by feeling young rather than just looking young!

### Age acceptance
You accept how old you are, perhaps because there is not much you can do about it. The difference between this and age irrelevance is that you feel as old as you are. This may result in you losing that "inner child" that is filled with zest and enthusiasm for the future.

How would you identify your views on aging based on these four approaches?

There is a difference for most people between their chronological age and their subjective age. In other words, "How old would you be if you didn't know how old you are?" As you think about your current age, how old do you actually feel at this very moment?

- ☐ Less than five years younger
- ☐ 10 years younger
- ☐ From 10 to 20 years younger
- ☐ More than 20 years younger

*Let me share a story…*

Not long ago, I had occasion to talk to a delightful woman who was 85 years old. She was very sharp and had a great sense of humour. You could see the sparkle in her eyes as she related her story to me. "Recently," she told me, "I was invited with my husband to our 45th high school reunion. My husband and I were high-school sweethearts, and had gone to the same school.

"When my husband told me about the reunion, my initial reaction was to say, 'No, I am not going.' After all, I had grown older and I was certain that no one would recognize me any longer. Also, I was certain that a lot of people that I wanted to see would, sadly, not be there.

"We went to the reunion and I was right—no one recognized me and I didn't recognize anyone else. After all, it had been 65 years since we had last been together. It was interesting, though, what happened at the reunion. The more we all talked and the more wine we drank, at the end of the night we were all 18 again!"

© MARK ANDERSON                                    WWW.ANDERTOONS.COM

"At my age my only comfort food is bran."

## What You Can Expect As You Get Older

Aging is accompanied by several physical changes that are a direct result of getting older. Some of these you can plan for, some you might prevent or forestall and some you can do nothing about.

*Here are some areas most commonly affected by aging:*

**Gradual sensory loss:** Unfortunately, aging will diminish our ability to see, hear, touch, taste and smell to the some degree. While not everyone loses abilities at the same pace, the chances are very good that you will experience some loss in more than one area.

These sensory losses affect people in different ways, but they can take away many of the pleasures of life. Imagine, for example, not being able to smell the flowers on a spring day, hear your grandchildren laugh or taste your favourite meal.

While cures are not available for most sensory losses, if you understand what happens in the aging process, you will be better able to adapt as opposed to allowing these changes to affect how you feel about life.

Sensory loss starts a lot earlier than you might think:

- Vision: mid-50s
- Hearing: mid-40s
- Touch: mid-50s
- Taste: mid-60s
- Smell: mid-70s

*Let's look at some specifics, again not to scare you but to make you aware.*

### Memory
Memory becomes less efficient with age, starting around age 50. A key is to keep the "circuits working" so that you are always exercising your mind.

### Vision
As we get older, the shape of our eye lens changes. Our pupils become smaller and our field of vision shrinks. Think in terms of driving at night, or distinguishing between light and dark. Studies suggest that an 80-year-old needs three times as much light as a 40-year-old in order to see properly, and yet many seniors do not compensate for loss of vision.

### Hearing
Much of our hearing loss comes from a decrease in the elasticity of the eardrum. Hearing loss can also lead to balance problems, associated with inner ear issues. "High tone deafness" is a common form of hearing loss, making high-frequency sounds harder to hear.

Hearing loss is not often given the importance it deserves; it can severely undermine our sense of well-being. A study in Canada found that hearing loss is the No. 1 contributor to depression in older adults. It is estimated that 30% to 50% of older Americans experience hearing loss sufficient to harm their social relationships.

### Touch
As our skin loses its elasticity, our sense of touch is compromised. We may not be able to feel pain, or do simple things such as picking up a coin or holding a pen properly.

### Taste and smell
Did you know that by age 80 you would only have one third of the number of taste buds that you had when you were 30? The main effect of this loss of taste is our ability to enjoy sweet or salty tastes. It also explains why so many older Americans believe that their food tastes bland and why they increase the use of salt and spices.

Our sense of smell also declines as we age, a key factor in our perception of taste due to the relationship between the two.

These are normal occurrences as you get older and it is appropriate to focus on them now when your faculties may still be in good shape. If you expect these to happen, you can make some adjustments.

Some other physical changes as you get older

### Cardiovascular
Generally, your heart gets slightly bigger as you age and your heart rate slows down; in addition, your blood vessels are less elastic and can cause your heart to work harder. This may lead to cardiovascular problems and high blood pressure. Your lungs slowly lose their ability to expand to the same extent as when you were younger.

### Bones, joints and muscles
Your bones are likely to lose density and shrink in size (which explains in part why we lose height as we get older). Your muscles, tendons and ligaments all lose their elasticity, often resulting in balance problems and lack of flexibility in your muscles and joints. In Canada today, one out of four women over age 60 have some form of osteoporosis while one in eight men are also affected.

### Skin
As you get older, your skin produces less oil. It also becomes thinner, less elastic and more prone to wrinkles. The sun is particularly bad for aging skin.

### Height

By age 80, you can lose up to two inches in height from age 50. This comes from changes in your posture, spinal cord and disks.

### ARE YOU HAVING FUN YET?

**Don't despair.**

There are things that you can do as part of your healthy aging routine to lessen some of the effects of the natural aging process.

## What Things Can You Control?

• **Include physical activity in your daily routine.** Try walking, swimming or other activities you enjoy. Regular moderate physical activity can help you maintain a healthy weight, lower blood pressure and lessen the extent of arterial stiffening.

• **Eat a healthy diet.** Choose vegetables, fruits, and whole grains, high-fibre foods and lean sources of protein, such as fish. Limit foods high in saturated fat and sodium. A healthy diet can help you keep your heart and arteries healthy.

• **Acknowledge that certain parts of you don't work as well as they used to**. Today, hearing aids are small and can be almost completely hidden in your ear. Eyeglasses and contacts will open up a whole new world for you.

• **Don't smoke.** Smoking contributes to the hardening of your arteries, and increases your blood pressure and heart rate. If you smoke or use other tobacco products, ask your doctor to help you quit.

• **Manage stress.** Have we talked enough about this yet? Stress can take a toll on your heart. Take steps to reduce stress—or learn to deal with stress in healthy ways.

• **Include vitamins in your daily regimen.** Calcium for bones and vitamin D for overall health are two important supplements. Also, vitamin B can help manage stress and vitamin C can reduce your risk of strokes.

• **Be active socially.** This will help you with mental acuity, memory and outlook. Join groups, be open to people, seek out new relationships.

• **Be active mentally.** Reading, crosswords, Sudoku and Luminosity are examples of ways that you can exercise your mind.

There is not only a difference between chronological and subjective aging, but also a difference between your actual age and "biological" aging. How you perceive the process of aging, your expectations and beliefs, how you experience time and how energetic you feel actually determine the biology of aging.

## Getting Older—It's All How You Frame It

There are several common challenges experienced by older people. Consider the following:

- Maintaining health and fitness
- Maintaining social networks and activities
- Feelings of sadness and loss
- Ensuring financial security
- Decreases in mobility
- An increased reliance on others

It is all how you frame the issues that you will face going forward. Some might argue that we should not have included information on the aging process—after all, you knew these things anyway, right? Were there any surprises that you hadn't observed in older people you know (or in yourself)?

A happy, healthy Second Life is going to be driven by how you frame things. Whether it is stress issues, health issues, relationships or financial issues, successful retirees look at life as "a glass half-full" and understand that it is all how you deal with the challenges!

"It's just that I've changed! I've grown! And you're still stuck in the past!"

## What Will You Do With This Information?

As you think about your plans for the future, what kinds of things can you do to help your mind and body respond to inevitable aging issues?

- ☐ See a doctor immediately and get a complete physical.
- ☐ Have a dietician review your diet.
- ☐ Visit a naturopath to review your vitamin regimen.
- ☐ Join a gym and do some cardiovascular and weight training.
- ☐ Engage a personal trainer.
- ☐ Set up a weight loss program and decide on a goal weight and strategy.
- ☐ Stop smoking.
- ☐ Review you alcohol intake and decide whether it needs to be changed.
- ☐ Start a walking, cycling or running routine.
- ☐ Engage a personal coach, psychologist or psychiatrist to help you with focusing on your mental process.
- ☐ Become more physically active.
- ☐ Engage in more activities that will strengthen your mind.

## DID YOU KNOW?

• Within six weeks of beginning to exercise, studies show a 100% to 200% increase in strength in men aged 60 to 70. And walking for 30 minutes, five days a week, can add more than seven years to your life, according to a recent Harvard University study.

• Research shows that some areas of the brain involved with memory and learning continue to produce new nerve cells every day.

• Energy levels in the body don't depend on age—they depend on your attitude and are influenced by the quality of your life. Meditation, restful sleep and exercise are the best ways to experience a joyful and energetic body.

• Epigenetics is a new field in the study of aging. New research has suggested that while our genetic code determines our longevity, healthy habits and mental attitude can actually help us turn on good genes and turn off bad genes!

• US has about one-fifth of the geriatricians it needs. There are only six geriatric doctors under the age of 35 in US. In Europe, geriatrics is second only to cardiology as a chosen specialty among doctors.

# PART 5

*YOUR RELATIONSHIPS
AND YOUR SECOND LIFE*

# CHAPTER 15
## *No Man (or Woman) is an Island*

### SOME THINGS TO CONSIDER:

• How much do you share your feelings, hopes and emotions with those you care about?

• Are your personal relationships supportive and fulfilling, or stressful?

• Have you talked about your Second Life plans with those who will share your journey?

• Are you contributing as much as you can to the relationships you find valuable?

This chapter focuses on your personal relationships and the fact that we are not meant to live alone. There are many benefits to close personal relationships, but often those benefits are overlooked as we get older. Of concern is the difficulty in forming new friendships, especially for men.

At a retirement session, the subject of relationships was discussed. One of the attendees, a single man in his early 50s, expressed his concern about relationships. As he put it, "I just don't like people. One of the things I am looking forward to the most in retirement is that I won't have to interact with people on a day-to-day basis."

Many in the room tried to convince him that his life would be better if he had other people in it. "What about your family?" someone asked. Another inquired if he had a childhood friend whom he still talks to, or perhaps a co-worker who he could sit down and have a beer with? When they received a negative response, the group was left to recognize his right to choose his own path.

## Why are relationships so important in your Second Life?

In your Second Life, your friends and family will provide you with much of your "quality of life." Think about the positives that your personal relationships provide you:

• Someone to share your emotions with (both positive and negative)
• Someone to listen to you and support you
• Someone to have fun with
• Someone to help you and someone for you to help
• Someone to provide you with advice

Obviously, the list could go on for many pages. Intuitively, we know that positive relationships make our lives better; our friends provide us with life happiness, self-esteem and an increased desire to take care of ourselves.

Researchers have drawn a link between life happiness and the close relationships that we enjoy. For example, U.S. researchers say "satisfaction with life was found to be related to experiences with family and friends— those with regular participation in one's life—and to be unrelated to those with whom contact is brief or irregular." (Hong and Duff, 1997)

Science also tells us that there is a direct relationship between the quality of our relationships and our ability to manage stress. In addition, new research suggests that the presence of a nurturing social network can slow the aging process, lower blood pressure and strengthen your immune system.

In Chapter 9, we examined the role that "connectedness" plays in the strengthening of a "hardy" personality. In Chapter 8, we focused on the concept of PERMA and the relationship between engagement and retirement happiness. We will revisit these again below.

## Relationships and health

A lot of research has been done on the health benefits of having a strong social network in later years. Studies have shown a direct correlation between the size of your social network and your longevity. A Swedish study found that only the correlation between our age and our health was as significant.

Researchers conducting a study for the Centre for Ageing Studies at Flinders University followed nearly 1,500 older people for 10 years. They found that seniors who had a large network of friends outlived those with the fewest friends by 22%.

Further, researchers at Brigham Young University and the University of North Carolina at Chapel Hill looked at a number of studies conducted in the developed world. The findings were clear: those with poor social connections had on average 50% higher odds of death in the study's follow-up period (an average of 7.5 years) than people with more robust social ties.

The authors of the study also commented that the boost in longevity because of a strong social network is the same as the difference between non-smokers and smokers!

While the research is in its early stages, scientists have discovered that:

• When we have close relationships with friends, we are more likely to take better care of ourselves.

• Close personal relationships actually lower our stress levels by producing both dopamine and serotonin to counterbalance negative hormones. Researchers also noted a drop in a patient's blood pressure when a close friend accompanied him or her.

• In another study in Sweden, researchers found that an individual over age 50 perceived less major stress events in his or life if there was a strong social network in place.

• Social networks can also boost the immune system. For example, a 2004 study at Carnegie Mellon University in the U.S. found that participants who were exposed to the cold virus and had a healthy and diverse social network were less likely to develop a cold than those with a weak social network.

"Well when *are* we going to be able to look back
on that and laugh?!"

## What Kinds Of Positive Relationships Contribute To Your Health?

The research says that nurturing, supporting relationships are more important to us than incidental contacts. But incidental relationships still have value to you if they contribute to your social engagement.

## There are several layers to our social network:

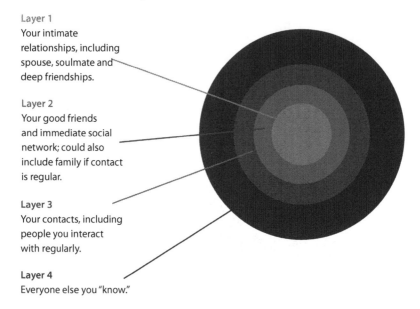

**Layer 1**
Your intimate relationships, including spouse, soulmate and deep friendships.

**Layer 2**
Your good friends and immediate social network; could also include family if contact is regular.

**Layer 3**
Your contacts, including people you interact with regularly.

**Layer 4**
Everyone else you "know."

The relationships at Levels 1 and 2 will have the most positive effect on your mental health. These are the nurturing, supporting relationships that we spoke of. People in Level 3 are those you work with, play golf or tennis with, interact at the club, etc. These are people you potentially could move into your Level 2 friendships if you choose.

## Introverts, Ambiverts and Extroverts

Our desire to socialize is considered to be one of the "big five" elements of personality. Psychologists say our attitudes toward socialization define us as being introverts, ambiverts or extroverts. As we mentioned earlier, not everyone is the same. There is a wide range of percentages to quantify each, but generally 15% of the adult population are true introverts, 15% are extroverts and the rest are ambiverts (or somewhere in the middle).

There is a social bias toward extroversion in that we tend to be drawn to those people who are outgoing and the life of the party. Often we consider introverts to "lack social skills." It is great to say, "you should go out and make friends," but that is easier said than done for introverts.

An **introvert** is a person who has a low need for socialization; true introverts tend to prefer less interaction with others and often do better academically. Note that introversion is not to be confused with shyness. Introverts prefer solitary pursuits such as fishing, kayaking alone, reading, etc. In fact, lots of social interaction can be considered stressful for introverts and doesn't always make them happy.

**Ambiverts** are more comfortable in social gatherings, and will interact with others and enjoy the contact. However, they often would prefer to leave the party and be by themselves, or in "safe" interactions with spouses or close friends.

**Extroverts** seek out new relationships and are happiest when they are able to share ideas with others. They strive to create relationships to feed their need for socialization. They get energy from other people and often are bored when they are by themselves.

## Are Extroverts Happier?

The research on this area is pretty clear: Happiness is positively (and significantly) correlated with extroversion. Extroverts are more optimistic and gain greater pleasure and positive reinforcement from their social activities. On the other hand, introverts do not gain as much pleasure or arousal from being alone. (Kuppens 2008 is a great study.) In short, extroverts will produce more dopamine and serotonin than introverts by doing what they like to do.

## What Does This Mean To Your Retirement?

We are not saying that you should become an extrovert. However, if you feel you are somewhere in the middle, we are going to give you some ideas on how to move "further to the right" on the continuum. If you are an introvert, we can't turn you into an extrovert, but if we could move you more to the right you may get more out of your retirement.

## The Challenge Of Making Friends

Making friends or building social relationships sounds easy, but for many people it is not. Men seem to be naturally predisposed to keeping their own counsel rather than sharing their innermost thoughts with one another. It's not that they can't make new friends; rather, they often don't recognize the need to do so. Also, people get busy and have other priorities that get in the way in very crowded calendars.

In retirement, some of those demands on your time are no longer there; this gives you the opportunity to create new relationships. While it sounds easy, you may have gone so long without building new relationships you may have forgotten how!

*Certain personality traits are needed to create social relationships:*
1. You have to see the value of social relationships.
2. You have to recognize the need to keep adding new relationships to replace those that you will inevitably lose.
3. You have to believe that you have value as a friend and something to offer someone else.
4. You have to like people and be open to interacting with them.
5. You have to be willing to start conversations and learn about others.

As you look at these five traits, how would you measure yourself? At the outset, we said that we were not going to tell you how to retire; we also pointed out later "you are who you are." If it were not in your personality to engage with others, would you be open to trying? If you don't see the value, can we convince you that this is as close to a "must" as we can suggest without telling you what to do?

If you are trying to create new relationships, here are some things you could do:

✔ Accept and extend invitations; find excuses to get to know other people. Make your first response "Yes" rather than "I am busy."

✔ Join a club or get involved in your community.

✔ Volunteer.

✔ Take up a new interest such as going back to school, joining a gym, visiting a senior centre, etc.

✔ Look for organizations in your community such as Meet Up, a meeting place for people who want to engage in a social or recreational activity but don't want to do it on their own. (Note: there is a Meet Up organization in most major centres in Canada.)

## Nurturing And Supporting Your Relationships

*Intimate relationships cannot substitute for a life plan. But to have any meaning or viability at all, a life plan must include intimate relationships.*

—**Harriet Lerner**

I have a good friend who I would say is one of my best friends. I have known him since I was eight years old and though he lives on the other side of the country, I try to keep in touch as much as possible. For us, Skype calls and regular emails have helped bridge the gap. I recognize that a relationship is "give and take." I never say, "Gavin hasn't called me in a while, therefore I am not going to call him until he does!" After all, this is a friendship, not a contest where we keep score.

As you move into this next phase of life, your nurturing and supporting relationships will add much enjoyment, good health and support. Relationships are give and take. While you may receive nurturing and support from your friends, are you providing the same to them?

From a health perspective, providing someone else with the benefit of your support provides you with satisfaction and a feeling of well-being.

*Here are some ways you can nurture your relationships in your Second Life:*

• Feel good about yourself and the value you bring to others.
• Don't judge others.

• Be positive and optimistic. People will pick up on that energy.

• Don't compete. Friendship isn't a one-up game where you are trying to outdo someone.

• Be a good listener. Sometimes people want to have someone to listen to them. You are a good friend if you can make them feel comfortable that you are there for them.

• Respect boundaries. Give your relationships space.

## Building A Social Support Network

The older we get, the more we have to depend on others. We will still have our advisors, physicians and professionals who we build relationships with. In fact, as we age we tend to develop deeper bonds with the people we are related to professionally. They make up an important part of our social network.

The rest of our social support network will come from people who will be there for us as we get older, including family members, friends and acquaintances who care about our well-being.

## The Dynamics Of Relationships In Retirement

We all have different personalities when it comes to our relationships and a brief understanding of these types may help you develop closer contacts. David McClelland from Harvard has identified three such personalities:

• Those people who view relationships as an opportunity to exert their **power** over others

• Those who view relationships as a way to gain **achievement**

• Those who look at relationships for the **affinity** with others

How would you describe yourself? For example, if you like power over others you should find ways in retirement to lead others, chairing your condo board, creating your own consulting business, teaching, etc.

On the other hand, if you like to achieve things through others, volunteering, participating in your community or joining a service club might be your thing.

Finally, if you like relationships for the affinity with others, you'll want to put yourself in as many places as you can where you can interact with others.

# Exercise

## Defining Your Relationships

If you had to assign the people you know to the four levels that we spoke of earlier, how would you do it? In the area below, look at your Level 1 to 3 relationships and identify those people who fit.

| Level 1 | Level 2 | Level 3 |
|---|---|---|
| These are your closest family, friends and spouse or partner. You share your deepest feelings with these people and consider them an integral part of your life. | These are the people you would call "friends." You may see them regularly and they are an important part of your social life. You could also include close friends who live elsewhere, if they don't fit into Level 1. There is an emotional attachment to them, though not to the same degree as Level 1. If you choose, you could put some family members here. | These are people you interact with regularly, at work, at the club or in the community. This level consists of your "relationships" as opposed just to "people you know." |
|  |  |  |

# Exercise

## Nurturing And Supporting Your Relationships

As you think about your relationships, we want you to look at why you placed them on the level you did and what kinds of things you can do to strengthen and support them. Think of the highlights of each relationship and how important they are to your life today and your Second Life.

| Relationship | Relationship Highlights: proximity, frequency, nurturing, caring, etc. | What can you do to strengthen and support this relationship? |
|---|---|---|
| Your spouse or partner | | |
| Your children | | |
| Your grandchildren | | |
| Your parents and in-laws | | |
| Your siblings | | |
| Your friends | | |
| Your work relationships | | |

Part 5: No Man (or Woman) is an Island

| Continued... Relationship | Relationship Highlights: proximity, frequency, nurturing, caring, etc. | What can you do to strengthen and support this relationship? |
|---|---|---|
| Your organizations, clubs, etc. | | |
| Other relationships (advisors, acquaintances, etc.) | | |

## What Will You Do With This Information?

*To strengthen my social network in my Second Life, I need to do the following:*

_____

_____

_____

_____

_____

_____

_____

_____

_____

_____

_____

_____

## DID YOU KNOW?

• Low social support is associated with higher levels of stress, depression, dysthymia and post-traumatic stress disorder and with increased morbidity and mortality from a host of medical illnesses. (Southwick et al., Clinical Psychology annual review, 2005)

• In a longitudinal study of 1,500 older Australians, researchers found that those who had extensive social networks outlived people who did not by 22%. (Giles et al., University of Adelaide)

• Social connections help relieve harmful levels of stress, which can harm the heart's arteries, gut function, insulin regulation and the immune system. (Harvard Health Publications, 2010)

• In their analysis of 148 studies of the relationship between healthy social relationships and longevity, Brigham Young researchers found that relationships were a direct contributor to the odds of a person living longer or dying earlier.

*Call it a clan, call it a network, call it a tribe, call it a family.*
*Whatever you call it, whoever you are, you need one.*

**"I'll tell you something, you're not the only one who is worried about you taking retirement."**

# CHAPTER 16
## Your Family And Your Retirement

### SOME THINGS TO CONSIDER

• What role will your family play in your retirement?

• What issues that may come from family will play a part in your retirement plans?

• Have you included your family in your discussion of retirement?

In this chapter, we look at the role that family plays in your next phase of life. There are few things in life more emotional than family and we examine both the positives and negatives that flow from our family connections. Also, we expand the definition of "family" to respect the deep emotional connections that we often have with our close personal friends.

"I must have won the lottery, my big shot
son is paying me a visit."

## The Importance Of Family Connections

The demands of family can increase during your retirement. Not only might there be financial demands or support to family members, but you could be involved in caring for a family member, helping with gardening or home maintenance for a parent, or babysitting grandchildren.

## Expanding The Definition Of Family

While family plays an important role in your Second Life, it can also cause you distress. Often, families may become dysfunctional over time and part of your retirement may involve refereeing conflicts between your adult children. Thankfully, many families are nurturing and supportive and can be the source of much happiness, involvement and satisfaction for you. Ultimately, your family may be in a position to provide you with much-needed support as you get older.

If we define "family" in emotional and psychological terms, its members would be those who know you the best and have your best interests at heart. By this definition, members may not even be related by blood; a daughter-in-law becoming best friends with her mother-in-law, childhood friends who are closer to you than your own family are just two examples of the expansion of the family definition.

Finally, who can say that pets aren't also "family"? In fact, pets can become an integral part of your retirement life, providing comfort, acceptance and humour!

## Involving Your Family In Your Planning

If you have adult children, it is often a good idea to sit down with them and share your vision of retirement. Let them in on your goals, how you want to spend your time and other issues surrounding the lifestyle that you want to live. The advantage of doing so is that they will have a better appreciation of how you wish to get the most out of this stage in life.

This may allow you to set out some guidelines about how your retirement life relates to your family and what you are willing or not willing to do.

*Some topics for discussion are:*

- Your travel ideas and plans
- Your involvement with grandchildren
- Moving, relocating or downsizing
- Health issues they should understand
- As much as you are prepared to share with them about financial issues that they should know about
- Contingency plans for unexpected events

Russell and Nicole had recently retired when we first met them at a workshop. While they felt they were ready for retirement, Nicole was concerned that there was too much distance between them and their children and grandchildren who lived about 1,600 kilometres away. She convinced Russell that they should move to be closer to the family, giving up relationships, a house they enjoyed and Russ's season tickets to his beloved college football team.

A year later, the couple moved back to their home city. While it was nice to interact regularly with family, this was beginning to become an everyday adventure; Russell and Nicole became the "go-to" child minders. "I didn't mind," says Nicole, "but I knew that my husband was miserable and I was now giving up my retirement plans and dreams for my family."

**Grandchildren** are a wonderful element of our lives and are often the focus of activities in retirement. Often, retirees will wish to move to be closer to family and grandchildren specifically. While this may work in certain situations, the challenge is what happens if your family moves? Are you going to follow them around Canada just to stay close? Would that fit your lifestyle? Would that fit theirs?

It is normally better not to be quick to move to be close to family unless you have physical or emotional needs that require their regular assistance.

## The Challenge Of Caregiving

Some retirees may become caregivers for a parent. There are many stories of people retiring to become full-time caregivers for a mother or father. One of the most-cited challenges that come with this responsibility is the toll that it takes on both mental and physical health.

Too often, caregiving falls on one family member more than on other siblings. This can create resentments on all sides; family members don't appreciate the sacrifice and the caregiver feels alone in taking on the burden.

It is a good idea to identify potential issues that may come up, particularly when it comes to dealing with aging parents. Family conferences provide opportunities to discuss issues before they arise and formulate plans. It is far too easy for caregiving responsibilities to derail the best retirement plans.

## What Will You Do With This Information?

### DID YOU KNOW?

• The majority of caregivers in the U.S. are female (65%), and more than 80% are caring for a relative or friend who is age 50 or older. (Family Caregiving Alliance)

• Many grandparents provide informal care for their grandchildren. Next to mothers, grandmothers are the most likely people to be caring for children, either full-time or part-time.

• 64% of boomers with children still have at least one child living at home.

# CHAPTER 17

## *I Married You for Love* (But Not for Lunch)

### SOME THINGS TO CONSIDER:

• What effect would 24/7 have on your relationship?

• How independent are you within your relationship?

• How will your roles in the household change in your Second Life?

• Are you on the same page when it comes to your retirement plans?

Often in our workshops, we focus on the issues that come up between couples as the result of the stressors in retirement. Many people approach this phase of life as if it will be save their relationships; others view it as the opportunity to draw even closer and look forward to devoting more time to each other. We give you this chapter to have you think about some of the relationship issues you may face.

Jim and Alison had recently retired and were looking forward to enjoying their lives after long careers and years spent raising a family. They became empty nesters and retired at the same time. It appeared that everything was lining up for a great transition into retirement.

Jim's idea of retirement was to involve himself with hobbies that he had neglected when he was working. Alison wanted to use this time to spend with her friends, to do some travelling and to go back to school. In fact, she had recently enrolled at a community college and was excited about learning new things.

The couple also renewed their marriage vows and spent a lot of time prior to retirement talking about how they could use this next phase of life to make their marriage even stronger.

## Conflicts To Avoid

### 1. Competing and conflicting plans

Do you think that couples should always have the same goals in retirement? A lot of couples strive to share the same goals, sometimes to the point where they stop leading independent lives and are now "joined at the hip." A couple that we know will not do anything separately: the spouses are together 24 hours a day, don't socialize and seldom find time to get some "alone time." Other couples hardly see each other at all: the husband is at the golf course every day while his wife does her own thing. They are like two ships passing in the night.

Our advice is to create some space in the relationship and pursue your own goals in addition to sharing goals with your spouse or partner. There should be an understanding of each other's goals and accommodation to allow your partner to pursue them, in much the same way as when you were working. . While you may not have the same goals as your partner, it might add to the quality of your Second Life to participate in one of your partner's goals or at least show support!

### 2. Independence and space

It is not just a couple who are retiring, but two individuals who are now moving into the next phase of their lives. Generally both are introspective, looking at their lives and their goals for the future. Each will have a different view of what self-actualization is and what he or she needs to do to achieve it.

In our workshops, we have each partner or spouse fill out his or her workbook independently and then compare notes afterwards. We recommend that both read this book in the same way. You might say, "But wait, we are soulmates and do everything together." What happens, though, if one person in the relationship ends up facing life as a single person? Try not to give up maintaining your own identity.

### 3. Pink jobs…blue jobs

Picture this. Husband is retired and wife is still working. Husband waits at home for his wife to return from work and cook him dinner! If there have been traditional responsibilities within the home, this phase of life can give you an opportunity to "reassign" some of the chores. For example, just because she cooked for 40 years doesn't mean that he can't cook in retirement. In fact, many men today have taken up cooking in their retirement as a hobby and delight in being able to create new things. Not only does this add to a sense of accomplishment, but also it takes some of the burden off the other spouse.

### 4. No communication

A major issue at this phase of life occurs when couples don't communicate. In fact, those couples that have never been strong communicators find that this problem is magnified in retirement. There are so many compromises, negotiations and plans that come with retirement that a lack of communication can cause unnecessary stress for the couple.

*We will talk more about communication in the next chapter.*

### 5. Health challenges

Roger and Marianne had been looking forward to their retirement for a long time. They had done everything possible to plan for their life after work; their money situation was going to work out better than they had expected, they had some clear goals on what they wanted to do and they had already booked their first major trip in their retirement. "Roger had received a set of golf clubs at his retirement dinner," Marianne remembers. "He was going to get back into golf and was also looking forward to doing some serious cycling now that he had time." Marianne also decided to take up golf and she had decided to enrol in some art history courses at a college in her city.

"We had everything that we needed to really start to enjoy our lives," says Marianne. "Then about a month after we retired, Roger started to complain about feeling tired and listless. We must have visited a half-dozen physicians before we got the definitive diagnosis. Two years later, Roger was confined to a wheelchair and I was a permanent caregiver for as long as he needed me."

### 6. Aging and Appearance

OK, we are all getting older and our appearance is going to change. Couples can encourage each other to practise healthy aging principles; in fact, that should be a big part of the Second Life plan and a fundamental value. However, we are not immune from some of the physical changes that aging will bring. We can resort to pills, creams, gels and tucks to make us feel young, or we can use our minds to see ourselves as young despite the physical changes.

Be kind and forgiving of your partner's changing appearance (and hope he or she does the same). Face the changes with humour.

## "He's getting old, his thoughts have turned from passion to pension."

### Strategies For Couples Entering Retirement

1 Agree on the goals that you have for this next phase. Don't assume that your goals will automatically become your partner's.

2 Give your partner some space. Respect his or her need for privacy and some "alone" time.

3 Encourage other friendships. No one can satisfy all of another person's needs.

4 Develop new routines, especially separate and shared activities.

5 Swap and share roles in the home and the marriage.

6 Be aware of physical and hormonal changes that may affect your partner's outlook.

## Grey Divorce

Divorce for aging Americans has been on the rise for the past two decades. In fact, in 2013 the average age of divorce for a man was 44.5 and 41.5 for American women. The divorce rate for those over the age of 50 has doubled in the past 25 years.

New studies suggest that there is a considerable impact on the health and well-being of American retirees who have gone through divorce later in life. Both men and women suffer emotionally, though it appears that men rebound quicker than women.

Retirement often results in a change in the dynamic between spouses or partners. Over the years, the demands of work and raising a family can cause a couple to go in different directions and evolve into different people. All of a sudden, retirement has thrown them together and forced them to get to know each other again.

Sometimes it works...and sometimes it doesn't. Retirement is a major stress point on a relationship because the concept of entering a new phase of life may mean re-examining all aspects. This includes personal relationships with your spouse and making a decision on whether you want to continue on with this person you have been married to for 30 years. As we said earlier, communication is the key.

Also, the glue of raising children together may lose its bond when the kids are gone. Partners who have stayed together until the children leave are now in a position to decide whether they too are ready to start a new life.

Dave, a client and friend, confided in me that he is concerned about his wife. "I am worried about Beth as we near retirement. I have all my friends at the club, and I am close with my brothers and their families. I have a life outside of each other and **interests that will continue into retirement.** Beth's life for many years has been the kids. When they are out of college and living their own lives, she won't have anything to fill her day and concern herself with. I am not sure where that will leave us, either.

"After a few more years of complaining
I think I may change my life."

## Emotional Challenges That May Come From Change

While mid-life crisis normally refers to the angst that both men and women go through as they hit their 40s and 50s, there can also be a similar crisis associated with the transition into retirement. Both men and women can experience feelings of inadequacy, irrelevancy or depression that follow the decision to leave work. This is mostly dependent on how they see themselves and whether they define their value by the work they do.

Tara was a recent participant in one of our workshops. As she sat and listened to the potential emotional challenges throughout a retirement transition, it finally hit her. "I never knew why my Mother was so depressed after she and my Dad retired. I know they are financially secure so I thought everything should be great. Instead, she was crabby and sat around the house all day. My Dad is off running around with his buddies all day, and she sits in the house by herself."

*Some things to watch out for:*
• Feelings of depression: This could include a change in sleep patterns, irritability, lack of energy, a sense of hopelessness or pessimism.

• A loss of interest in things that were once important: This might be a hobby or activity that they no longer pursue, a lack of willingness to do things, no interest in socializing.

• Anger or dissatisfaction with your spouse: Remember that the retirement transition can be hard on people who now feel helpless. There is a tendency to blame a spouse or to find fault in your mate to help you feel better about yourself.

• Inability to make decisions about the future: This can be a withdrawal from the planning process or a lack of optimism about the future. Feelings of disorganization, a lack of goals or a sense of inevitability can turn a normally optimistic "take-charge" person into a couch potato.
Differences in how men and women view the future

• Men are much more likely to build a plan for retirement on their own than to seek advice. In fact, more than half of men surveyed in a major American study in 2010 preferred to strike out on their own when it came to retirement planning, versus just one third of the women surveyed. Does this represent male ego at work, or does it suggest that men are far more likely to engage in financial plans?

• Women will be more likely to miss their workplace than men. A new British study suggests that work may actually provide a greater sense of purpose and social opportunities for women than for their male counterparts. Retirement can bring with it a sense of useful purpose.

• Women are more likely to be on their own than men. This makes the sense of isolation even worse because the workplace once provided social support.

• Men are generally either working or playing. Retirement then becomes a time of leisure to the point that some men will actually resent any discussion that says that leisure may not be what they thought it was (see our discussion of the paradox of leisure in Chapter 20) Women, on the other hand, are more likely to do the same kind of things in retirement that they did before and have simply reapportion their time.

## What Will You Do With This Information?

• What issues do you and your spouse need to talk about?
• What steps will you take to improve your communication if you need to?
• Do you have an appreciation of your spouse's goals for the future? What can you do to share in those or step aside to provide space?

## DID YOU KNOW?

• It is estimated that the standard of living for a woman in her first year after a divorce will drop by 45%. (BMO Retirement Institute)

• In a American study of couples who had not yet retired, 38% of men surveyed said that, in retirement, they wanted to spend more time with their spouses. Only 9% of wives wanted to spend more time with their husbands!

# CHAPTER 18
## Essential Conversations for Couples

## SOME THINGS TO CONSIDER

- Do you and your spouse communicate about your plans?
- Are you on the same page when it comes to your retirement?
- Are there "hot button" issues that you do not talk about?
- Are there family issues that cause conflict between the two of you?

We wrote this chapter because, frankly, many couples don't talk when it comes to retirement. One of the most important keys to a strong retirement relationship is communication. The challenge has been that up to retirement there was a different dynamic in the relationship that often interfered with communication. In retirement this is crucial and we will examine some of the reasons why.

## The Importance Of Communicating With Your Spouse Or Partner

Experience tells us that many couples do not share their feelings, hopes and concerns about the future with those who will share their lives. They take for granted that they are both "on the same page" when it comes to how they want to spend the rest of their lives.

Françoise and Jean-Luc were approaching the end of their work careers and had met several times with their financial advisor to discuss retirement. Normally, these conversations consisted reviewing their financial plan and looking at some financial projections to see how long their money would last, given what they thought would be their lifestyle. Jean-Luc was not even sure that he was going to retire, though he hadn't discussed this in detail with his wife. Françoise had her mind set on buying a condo at a gated community in Tampa, Fla., where they had spent many holidays.

For the past year, she had contacted real estate agents and set her plan to buy their retirement dream in motion. Jean-Luc says that he went along with it because he always thought that her dreams would cool and that she would have second thoughts. "I never really thought that we would go through with it," he commented to his advisor. "When we were talking about a retirement that was five years away, that felt like a lifetime to me. I would agree to anything she wanted if I didn't have to act on it immediately. I should have said something earlier about wanting to stay in my job past the point when I could take retirement. It's just that I didn't want to upset her dream."

Intuitively, we know how important communication is between spouses; in reality, however, sharing ideas, fears, dreams and stressors can become more difficult over time. Relationships that have always flourished because of the communication between partners will continue to nurture and grow in Second Life. Those relationships that did not have strong communications between partners will experience additional stress in retirement.

This is a period of life where having someone to share the joys and burdens makes handling the stress a lot easier. Consider a relationship where there is not a strong sense of a shared life:

John, 49, is looking at a new beginning. Currently employed as an engineer with a local municipality, he is seriously considering leaving his job and starting his own consulting company. "I have a couple of friends in my field who are already working as consultants and rave about the freedom that their life provides them," he told me at one of our workshops. "I am getting really excited about the possibility of taking control of my work life and becoming my own boss."

John's wife, Margaret, fears her husband may have "bit off more than he can chew." "I like the fact that he has a secure job and that our health insurance is paid for" s,he told me later. "I don't want him to leave his work and I certainly do not want to worry about whether we have enough money to maintain our lifestyle."

In the course of my conversation with both John and Margaret, it became apparent that each was living a separate life and that there wasn't a lot of conversation between them about future plans. Margaret had always been the "'supportive" wife, which in reality meant that John ran things and that she was expected to go along with whatever he did.

"This is my life too," she said. "If he wants to put our lifestyle at risk, he can damn well do it on his own!"

# Mutual respect made them a top Senior Mixed Doubles team.

## The Essential Conversations

There are a number of areas where couples need to have the conversation in order to come to some agreement. Nobody is saying that you have to agree on everything or even have the same views, but at some point there has to be a meeting of the minds on these areas:

### 1 Financial planning

Did you know that women are less likely to engage in financial planning than men? While the numbers suggest that men tend to have more familiarity with the financial planning process, the caveat is that this familiarity may come from their exposure to investing in the stock market; many equate financial planning with investment management and the two are *clearly not the same.*

There is more than a 90% chance that at some point, the woman will be the sole financial decision-maker in the household, according to a study conducted by Prudential in 2011. This alone makes the case that most women need to engage in some form of financial planning.

There are some specific issues that will affect American women that may not be as big a planning factor for men. Here are some things to consider in your discussions:

**Women live longer.** Women now outlive men by an average of six years. This means they will have to save more because they'll have more years of retirement to fund. Women represent just over half (50.5%) of the total American population. However, they represent 53% of the overall population in the 65-74 cohort, 60% in the 74-85 cohort and 70% of the population over age 85. In fact, 80% of centenarians are women.

**Women tend to be the major caregivers for elder parents.** Caregiving and managing parental assets will affect both men and women but will likely be more relevant to a woman than a man.

**Women tend to have longer retirements,** simply because they live on average six years longer than their husbands. From a purely financial-planning perspective both men and women need help preparing for a long retirement. The reality, however, is many women will need even more help to handle those extra years, given their prospects for greater longevity, a lack of pension benefits, etc.

**Women are more likely to live alone in retirement.** Issues such as household budgeting, health care, financial planning, legacy issues and investment management will be increasingly taken on by women.

**Women will take an active role in family finances in the future**. Increasingly, more women control the family finances. According to the National Center for Women and Retirement Research in New York, between 80% and 90% of all women in the U.S. will be the sole decision-make about their family finances at some point in their lives. Our advice has always been that the woman in the relationship should be prepared to take over family finances at a moment's notice—she is doing herself no favours by sticking her head in the sand.

## 2 Health challenges
It is easy to avoid discussions on how to handle health challenges that may affect a marriage or partnership. We don't want to talk about the negative aspects of aging.

Couples should discuss the what-ifs and make sure that they are on the same page when it comes to dealing with a health issue. Topics such as mental or physical incapacity, poor health habits, caregiving, depression, and substance abuse are just some of the issues that can arise at this point in life.

As couples make plans for the future, all of the above should be "on the table" with plans made to handle both the expected problems and strategies to address the unexpected.

## 3 Activities and leisure

Your Second Life is a time to do things that you have always wanted to do; this could include engaging in new activities, your bucket list items or simply how you want to spend you free time. On a weekend or a holiday, this is probably not an issue. However, in retirement, there has to be some give and take, and coordination in order to show respect for your partner's plans.

We are big believers in the independence of the partners. You should have your own activities, separate from those of your spouse or partner. However, you should also find activities that you can do together, including flow activities and new activities.

## 4 Moving

Often couples don't agree on whether their home fits the needs of their Second Life. They may differ on how attached they are, or what works for the lifestyle that they envisage. For example, one might want to downsize so that she can spend less time worrying about a house with rooms they never use; the other might like the house, enjoy the yard work and think of the home as the symbol of his success.

Another issue that might arise is the desire of one to move to be closer to family, while the other might have a different idea of the ideal retirement home. The challenge is for each party to understand the other and negotiate a compromise that works for both. This is not the best time for one to impose his or her will on the other, as that will only lead to problems later.

Moving is one of the most stressful things that can happen in retirement, and its negative impact is often greatly underestimated. For example, moving to a new place throws a wrench into established routines; even the act of moving around the house can no longer be done on "autopilot."

## 5 Timing of retirement

A question often asked is, given the choice, who should retire first? Is there a rule of thumb to determine what would happen if:

• One retires before the other
• Both retire together
• One decides to never retire
• One decides to work part-time
• One decides to build a new business

The conversation between spouses or partners should focus on the plans that each has for retirement. If one partner is more of a "self-starter" and has plans to go out and do something in retirement, this will be less of a stressor on the other partner. However, if the retiring partner clearly has no idea what he will do and the other partner is worried that he will sit around all day, then there is an issue.

## 6 Family

In our experience, couples don't pay enough attention to the role that family plays in retirement. This is particularly true when there are grandchildren involved or if adult children have unexpected needs that may draw on your resources. As we have noted earlier, this is your retirement—not theirs. A conversation about the issues that may arise will help avoid conflicts or misunderstandings later.
*Here are some topics to consider:*

• How to deal with family requests for money
• Caregiving for parents
• Being obligated to host or visit family
• Child-minding
• Adult children moving home
• Adult children's marital breakups

## 7 Estate planning

A frank conversation about "what happens when" is important at all times and should never be ignored. When you consider the number of Americans who don't have up-to-date wills and instructions, it would make sense for couples to discuss the important issues.

In this age of the nuclear family, clear understandings about disposing of assets, fairness and provision for children from previous marriages, etc., should all be part of the discussion.

Finally, a couple should be clear with each other what what each would like to happen in the final days of life, and also be clear about how each would to have his or her final wishes carried out.

## What Will You Do With This Information?

• What conversations do you need to have right now?

• Would your spouse or partner be able to take over immediately if he or she had to?

• Are you both on the same page regarding family, home and lifestyle?

# CHAPTER 19
## Facing Your Second Life on Your Own

### SOME THINGS TO CONSIDER:
• Would your Second Life be happier with someone in your life or on your own?
• If you became "suddenly single," would you be able to make the adjustment? How long do you think it would take?
• Is your social network strong enough to provide you with the support you need?

The purpose of this chapter is to pose what-if questions to those currently in relationships, as well as to ensure that we address specific issues faced by those who are single. While these are not always easy issues to discuss, the fact is that there is a very good chance that at some point one person in the relationship will be on his or her own. Also, to ignore the needs of those who are single further supports the idea that retirement is only about couples—not only is that not true, but also not fair.

I met a woman at one of our workshops who gave me a perspective on relationships that I had not considered. Marian was in her early 50s and had been widowed five years earlier. Her children had families of their own and lived on the west coast, two time zones away. Marian confided that she didn't keep in touch as much as she might and that she had not spoken to her oldest son in four years because of some disagreement that seemed small to her now. Since her husband's death, Marian had immersed herself in her work as an accountant at a hotel and had grown apart from the friends that she had with her husband. "I don't really socialize much at work," she said.

"Most of the people I work with are considerably younger. Besides, by the time that I am done my week's work, I am ready to go home and take the weekend to relax." Marian's relaxation didn't include a lot of friends or family. "I guess that it is my choice," she commented. "I feel like such a hermit these days." Marian acknowledged that she hadn't "'worked" on her relationships. On the verge of retirement, however, she was becoming concerned about being alone. "When I come home at night, whom am I supposed to talk to about my day?" she mused. "If I die in the middle of the night, how long will it be before someone finds me? Who will look after my cats? Whom can I confide in when I am not feeling well, or when I am well? Frankly, it never occured to me that I might die alone."

## The Importance Of Being A Self-Starter

We talked earlier (Chapter 8) about the role that optimism and being a self-starter plays in your mental health and outlook. As a single person at this stage of your life, you will find it far easier to take control and "make things happen." Self-starters don't depend on others for support as they strive to achieve their goals, believing that, if they had to, they could do it themselves.

If you have been single for a long time, you probably have already recognized this. However, for those retirees who become "suddenly single," it is a difficult adjustment. For example, you don't want to socialize because you don't want to be thought of as a "third wheel," or you wait at home for the phone to ring for someone to get you out into the world.

Self-starters are people who have hardy personalities and believe that they have control over their own lives. They seek to control whatever they can, including socializing with others if they want to. They have decided that they will make the best out of their lives and don't feel sorry for themselves.

## The Role Of Your Social Network In Your Retirement

The stronger your social network, the easier it is for you as a single person. Again, a man who is on his own may not have the kind of social network that he needs for nurturing and support. This may explain why a man who is divorced or bereaved is more likely to form a new relationship than a woman would.

Your social network can become a surrogate family if you find yourself on your own. Not only can your friends help you through the rough patches, but they can also act as sounding boards and provide emotional support as you adjust.

## Developing Your Social Network As A Single Person

Service clubs and other community organizations will not only give you the opportunity to contribute to your community but will also allow you to develop new relationships. The workplace has always been a great place to build relationships because of shared goals and teamwork. You can gain similar benefits through volunteer work with such organizations as:

- Kinsmen and Kinettes
- Shriners
- Rotary
- Altrusa

### Strategies for singles in retirement

- Social networks become a major source of support and family replacement.

- The workplace provides many positives for singles from a support perspective.

- Successful singles in retirement tend to be self-starters.

- Don't discount the possibilities of future relationships (platonic or otherwise).

- Take advantage of the opportunities available to singles (travel, clubs, social organizations, Meet Up etc.).

## Exercise

### Your social network today

If you are single today or find yourself on your own, here is a quick assessment of the strength of your social network. Rank your life on a scale of 1 (low) to 5 (high) to indicate how you feel about your social support network in each situation.

| | |
|---|---|
| 1 - People don't come to visit me as often as I would like. | |
| 2 - I often need help from other people but can't get it. | |
| 3 - I seem to have a lot of friends. | |
| 4 - I don't have anyone who I can confide in. | |
| 5 - I have no one to lean on in times of trouble. | |
| 6 - There is someone who can cheer me up when I am down. | |
| 7 - I often feel very lonely. | |

| | |
|---|---|
| 8 - I enjoy the time I spend with the people who are important to me. | |
| 9 - When something's on my mind, just talking with the people I know can make me feel better. | |
| 10 - When I need someone to help me out, I can usually find someone. | |
| My overall perceived level of social support (average 1-10) | |

### Scoring this exercise:

1. Add up your scores in the statements above and then divide by 10 to get an average.

2. If you scored between 4-5, your social network appears to be strong

3. If you scored between 3-4, you may wish to do some more work to strengthen your social network

4. If you scored less than 3, you run the risk of not having as strong a social network as you will need to enjoy retirement on your own.

## DID YOU KNOW?

• A September 2011 report from the MetLife Mature Market Institute and Scripps Gerontology Center found that women are more likely than men to be widowed, divorced, or otherwise live alone.

• A 2011 New England study of men and women over the age of 100 found that a significant number of women over that age had never been married.

# PART 6

"I always hoped retirement would look like this."

## *ENJOYING YOUR LIFESTYLE*

# CHAPTER 20
## Second Life Leisure

### SOME THINGS TO CONSIDER:
• What you will be doing in this next phase of your life?
• What does leisure "24/7" really mean?
• What defines fulfilling use of your time (vs. time-filling)?
• What new things would you like to start?

Rick, 56, has recently retired from his job as a teacher and is looking forward to his life in retirement. He always wanted to travel, and both he and his wife Helen, 49, now empty nesters, want to use this time in their lives to travel to faraway places they have always longed to visit. "Rick insisted on buying a motorhome," said Helen at one of our workshops. "His view is that we will simply point the truck south and go wherever the road takes us." Helen realizes, however, that retirement means more than just travelling aimlessly in the motorhome or taking trips abroad. "After all," she says, "we still have to live our lives here. I'm not sure that Rick has really thought any further about our retirement plans outside of travel and finances."

Leisure is a fundamental human need. We use it to recharge our batteries, to act as a diversion in our lives, to create excitement and anticipation, and simply to rest and contemplate. Research tells us that regularly having fun is one of the five central factors in leading a satisfied life. Individuals who spend time having fun are 20% more likely to feel happy on a daily basis and 36% more likely to feel comfortable with their age and stage in life. (Lepper, 1996)

Things change, however, when leisure becomes the central focus. By its very nature, leisure loses its lustre when it is the norm rather than a diversion in our lives. And if the idea of leisure translates into "not having to do anything," it can produce stress "underload"—a lack of stimulation that can produce the same type of stress symptoms as stress "overload."

We should define leisure, however, because the concept as leisure as a break from work is more akin to the Protestant work ethic than to reality. Leisure in our discussion refers to the time when we have the freedom to do what we want. *Leisure can be divided into three different types:*

• Enjoyable activities— activities undertaken for the fun of doing them
• Engaging activities — activities that cause you to think or use your skills and strengths to accomplish a task
• Meaningful activities — those activities that enable you to build on the values you hold

## How Do You Want To *Feel* About Leisure In Retirement?

In our experience, leisure is one of the most misunderstood concepts among retirees. One reason is that leisure is seen as a break from work. When you were working, leisure was a compact length of time when you recharged your batteries and tried to fit as much as you could into two days or three weeks.

## Is Every Day Really Saturday?

Several years ago, a young entrepreneur in Canada wrote a book entitled *Every Day is Saturday*. The book was about his move to self-employment and how to free up self-imposed constraints to live the life you really want.

Some retirement speakers then hijacked the concept of 'Every Day is Saturday' to describe retirement as an extended day off work or long weekend. Just think: no more work, no more demands and a life of perpetual leisure. In fact, why not consider retirement a 30-year-long weekend?

Your Second Life is a time to do a lot of things that will add to your life enjoyment. Throughout this book, we have identified many things that will help you have the most fulfilling retirement possible. Ideally, this life would be full of challenge, satisfaction, achievement and purpose; however, to have that life, you need to change your view of retirement as an extended holiday. It is not just your job situation that has changed; it is your excitement for the opportunities that retirement can provide you.

However, there are still people who plan for retirement as if they are planning for a vacation. They have a list of places they are going to visit, things they are going to purchase, and hobbies they will take up. Their view of retirement is that leisure is its own reward.

## The Paradox Of Leisure

"I can hardly wait until the day I retire," said Bob during a workshop discussion. "After years of commuting and working, I am going to sit back, relax and just enjoy all my free time."

For many who are contemplating retirement, the idea of *free time* and leisure as the ultimate reward is ingrained. "Just think. Every day is Saturday and if you want to take a holiday for three months you can just do it!"

Not everything, however, is as it appears. Take the concept of free time. Most Americans who work in traditional jobs enjoy regular time off from work and relish holiday times with extended periods of free time—time to pursue fun and carefree activities. In truth, however, most of us have a myriad of weekend and vacation demands that challenge both our free time and our energy.

Between family commitments, errands and chores, special events, driving, exercise, spiritual observances and, of course, sleeping and eating, real "free time" is rare. Yet, despite the illusion of free time, we still look forward to our weekends and holiday time as valued breaks from the routine of work.

We can also look forward to our time off as a stress reliever. In our free time, we can assume diverse and enriching life roles, and let go of those work roles that may be unrewarding, tension-filled or harmful to our self-image. In fact, someone leaving the workplace may view retirement as just one long and well-deserved break. Since the idea of a break from daily routine is so attractive, then the idea of a perpetual break must be a very good thing, right?

Well, the question is, "If you have leisure 24/7 for the rest of your life, where is your 'break'"?

The paradox of leisure is that "too much of a good thing" can undo the very reason why it was a good thing in the first place! Too much leisure can produce feelings of monotony and restlessness and, in turn, lead to "organ recitals"—an endless recounting of health issues or obsessing over money, house repairs, physical signs of aging, etc.

So instead of viewing retirement as an unending life of free time, we suggest you envision and plan your Second Life as a mix-and-match journey that weaves together fulfilling activities with new adventures and, of course, luscious, carefree leisure time!

Ellen: "I have heard people say that if you retire, you are checking out of life—that retirement is 'death.' Well, as a 62-year-old retiree, I think I'm more active today than I ever was when I was working! I use my time to pursue those interests and activities that I envisioned doing and now my life is quite fulfilling! My weeks are filled with volunteering, social gatherings with friends, travelling, crafts and taking classes in everything from gardening to making beer to singing! I also give myself a daily dose of free time—time for just 'puttering around.' It's as valuable to me now as it was when I was working, but it wouldn't work as a steady diet!"

## "Perhaps you can tell me how many nights in the week you plan to go clubbing?"

### 'Free' Time – Fulfilling vs. 'Time-Filling'

There is a big difference between "time-filling" activities and "fulfilling" activities. As you look at this next phase of your life, what kinds of things do you want to spend your time on? Let's face it—one of the goals (and advantages) of your Second Life is living this life on your terms, gaining more control over how you use your time and invest your energy.

At a recent workshop, we heard two retirees remark on how busy their retirements were. "I just don't know where the time goes," commented John, 66. "I always seem to be busy doing something and the time just flies by." Margaret, 60, agreed, adding, "I thought I would be bored with the extra time, but I find myself wishing I had more time in the day!" On the surface, John and Margaret had no trouble filling their days; the difference came when we asked each of them if they were doing what they really wanted to do. John replied, "I don't seem to get to the things that I thought I would. I keep putting things off in order to attend to the day-to-day stuff. I don't feel all that organized and I am actually not pursuing those interests that I thought I would be when I was contemplating retirement."

On the other hand, Margaret felt that she was on track and engaging in many of the activities she had set out to pursue when she transitioned into retirement. "You really have to be organized," she told us. "I make sure to prioritize the things that I really want to do before I use up my time on things that are not as important to my overall happiness. In fact, I think that I am much more organized now than I was when I worked, mostly because I don't want to waste any time!"

A Snapshot of Time in Retirement

*You will never find time for anything. If you want time, you must make it.*

**— Charles Buxton**

There are 168 hours in a week. You sleep for roughly 56 hours of that time, which leaves you with 112 hours to fill. If you are working today, your work commitment takes up about 55 hours, leaving you with 57 hours to do things with your family and pursue your hobbies. (We know that *your* work takes up far more time than that today, but please play along so that we can illustrate the point!)

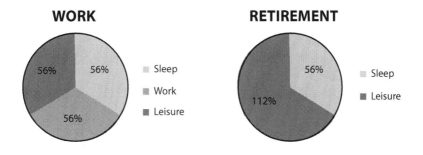

If your retirement simply means that you have walked away from work, one of the results is that you have added around 55 hours each week (or 11 hours a day, five days a week) to your "free time." Outside of sleep, it's all free time. You don't have to be anywhere, do anything or answer to anyone if you don't want to. What are you going to do with all of your time?

## Valuing Your Time

It is normal to think of retirement as a stage of life where you are no longer a prisoner of time. As one participant in our workshops said, "I have been tied to a clock since I started school. I no longer want to care about what time it is unless I have to be some place."

Earlier, we talked about the need to control the things that you can control. This creates structure in your life and can relieve the stress that comes from not feeling "grounded." A good way to do this is to keep a calendar of your events, write a diary of important events in your life and value the time you have.

After all, if you have been "tied to a clock" for many years, simply to decide to walk away from that control may cause you unnecessary stress in retirement.

## The Concept Of 'Flow' Activities

"Jack is a neighbour of ours and has been retired for the past t10 years. His hobby is fixing old cars, and one car in particular has taken a lot of his time. In his garage is a 1972 Camaro Sports Coupe. He bought the car with the idea that he would restore it; we often see him out in his garage working on the car, installing one thing or another. While the car has been lovingly restored, it still has not left the garage. When we asked Jack when he was going to take it out on the road, he was noncommittal. We got the impression that he would work on that car forever, that finishing it would end his enjoyment!"

Psychologist Mihály Csíkszentmihályi first wrote about the idea of "flow" activities when he and his researchers studied artists who "lost themselves" in their work. He noted that there are activities that most enjoy that take us to a new level psychologically. In fact, the concept of flow is one of the foundations of positive psychology.

We have many terms for "flow" activities, such as:

- "In the moment"
- "In the zone"
- "Lost in my work"
- "I am on a roll"
- "He was 'on fire'"

When you are involved in a flow activity, there is no room in your mind for anxiety, depression or doubt. You feel as if you have total control over what you are doing and you lose track of time as you are doing it.

The reward for the flow activity is more often "the journey" rather than the "destination." Our reward comes from being in the zone rather than accomplishing the end result.

Flow occurs when we are able to direct all of our attention to one activity as opposed to dividing it up between competing demands. The enemies to flow are apathy, boredom and frustration. In fact, flow activities are seen as important stress relievers because they eliminate (if only for a short time) negative or stressful thoughts that cause us to worry.

*Researchers at Indiana University found that the following psychological changes take place when we are involved in these kinds of activities:*

- We feel in control of our own actions, even if it is a potentially dangerous activity.
- We have a general feeling of well-being.
- We have an altered sense of time.
- There is a merging of action and awareness.
- There is an integration of mind and body.
- We can gain an understanding of true self and self-integration.
- We have a sense of our place in the universe and oneness of nature.

*Some Examples of Flow Activities*

| | | |
|---|---|---|
| • Reading | • Bicycling | • Playing music |
| • Writing | • Hobbies | • Gardening |
| • Exercise | • Housecleaning (really!) | |
| • Meditation | • Golfing (on a good day) | |
| • Painting | | |

## Flow Doesn't Have To Be A Solitary Activity!

Group activities can also create flow within the group as the participants become engaged in a task, a game or an activity. *For example:*

- Family game night
- Dancing
- Conversations
- Joke-telling
- Volunteering
- Competitions such as golf and tennis
- Trekking or hiking

## Giving Back—Volunteering In Retirement

There are lots of opportunities to volunteer your time and honour your feelings of altruism. There are other reasons why you should consider it:

- Developing a social network
- Using your strengths and transferable skills from work
- Creating a workplace replacement
- Using it to create structure in your life
- Varying your leisure activities to include volunteering
- Providing yourself with personal satisfaction
- Providing a source of achievement in your life

## Exercise

## What Brings You Joy?

As you consider the concept of flow activities, what kinds of things can you do in this next phase of life to put yourself "in the zone," relieve stress and "get away from it all"? These could be activities that you are already doing but perhaps don't have enough time to do more of.

# Exercise

## Your Time Management Habits Today

What challenges do you have when it comes to time management? The exercise below will give you a quick snapshot of your current skills/views. Tick the box that applies to you after each statement and then add up your score at the bottom.

| | never 1 | seldom 2 | sometimes 3 | usually 4 | always 5 |
|---|---|---|---|---|---|
| 1. I feel that I am an organized person and that I plan ahead as much as possible. | | | | | |
| 2. I set aside time on a regular basis to do the things that I most want to do. | | | | | |
| 3. I am able to accomplish the things that I want on a time schedule that I have set for myself. | | | | | |
| 4. I believe that managing my time is an important element of my life and will be in the future. | | | | | |
| 5. I have as much free time as I need to enjoy the things that I love about life. | | | | | |
| 6. I take time on a consistent, regular basis to keep up with my emails, pay bills, do banking, attend to personal needs, etc. | | | | | |
| 7. I recognize how quickly time moves and I try to "get things done" while I can. | | | | | |
| 8. I am able to prioritize my time so that I can focus on the most important things first. | | | | | |

| | never 1 | seldom 2 | sometimes 3 | usually 4 | always 5 |
|---|---|---|---|---|---|
| 9. I keep a "to do" list or a calendar to keep me organized and I review it regularly. | | | | | |
| 10. I do not waste my time on things that do not contribute directly to my quality of life. | | | | | |

Total  _____

## Scoring this exercise:

*If you scored:*

**Less than 29:** You may not be in control of your time management and find that you have challenges accomplishing the things that you want to do on a timely basis.

**30-39:** You have some success in managing your time and you are aware of the things that you should be doing to maintain control.

**More than 40:** You have few problems with time management. This will be an important strength as you enter your Second Life.

# Exercise

## An Average Week In Your Retirement

As we noted earlier, the average week has 168 hours. Think about an average week in retirement when you are at home just living your life. How will you spend your time? This is a great exercise to get you thinking about how you might apportion your time.

| Day | Sleep | Family focus | Work focus | Personal focus | Friend focus | Community focus |
|---|---|---|---|---|---|---|
| Monday | | | | | | |
| Tuesday | | | | | | |
| Wednesday | | | | | | |
| Thursday | | | | | | |
| Friday | | | | | | |
| Saturday | | | | | | |
| Sunday | | | | | | |
| Totals: | | | | | | |

*Include spirituality, meditation, fitness, personal activities, and hobbies in the "Personal focus" category.*

## Incorporating New Activities Into Your Retirement

What kinds of new things do you think that you might like to do in your retirement that fit into the concept of flow? Remember, these things don't just "happen" and the concept of flow suggests that you have some mastery over the activity; that probably means that "golfing" may not immediately become a flow activity if you are frustrated every time you tee it up!

# Exercise

## My Current Flow Activities

These activities are not meant to be a comprehensive list of future activities you want to start or expand, just a starting point! As you look at your entries ask yourself:

• How am I going to free up more time to do these?
• Why am I not spending more time on them now?
• How will I prioritize each one in my Second Life?

|   | Activity | What do I like best about it? |
|---|----------|-------------------------------|
| 1 |          |                               |
| 2 |          |                               |
| 3 |          |                               |
| 4 |          |                               |
| 5 |          |                               |
| 6 |          |                               |

|   | New Activities that may create 'flow |
|---|--------------------------------------|
| 1 |                                      |
| 2 |                                      |
| 3 |                                      |
| 4 |                                      |
| 5 |                                      |
| 6 |                                      |

# "Now you can write your epic novel about bug control."

## What Will You Do With This Information?

### Strategies for Change

• Identify and expand your list of leisure activities that recharge your batteries and bring enjoyment to your life.

• Pay yourself first. Prioritize and set aside time for these enjoyable activities before you undertake other obligations. While you may be committed to your work or to your free time, ensure that you schedule time for those activities that can revitalize you and make your life happier.

• Don't take time for granted. "Someday" is not a day of the week! And regardless of how urgently your mobile phone is ringing, you can choose to turn it off. Remember, you can't save, hoard or overspend time. Time doesn't fly—it moves at a fixed rate, and we have all there is! So, make your time count now — and in your Second Life.

• Create a balanced approach to leisure—even if it means taking a risk! Don't be afraid to experiment with new activities or to rediscover activities you haven't done in years. Surprise yourself! You are never too old to dive into activities in any of the areas of leisure we listed. What is one step you can take today to make your leisure time more enjoyable or meaningful?

## DID YOU KNOW?

• Historical sources suggest that Michelangelo may have painted the ceiling of the Vatican's Sistine Chapel while in a flow state. It is reported that he painted for days at a time, and he was so absorbed in his work that he did not even stop for food or sleep until he reached the point of passing out. After this, he would wake up refreshed and, upon starting to paint again, re-enter a state of complete absorption. (Wikipedia, 2013)

• Boomers volunteer at a higher rate than previous generations did at the same age, and are projected to increase volunteer rates by 50%.

# CHAPTER 21
## Balancing Your Leisure in Retirement

### SOME THINGS TO CONSIDER:
- What defines a *fulfilling* use of your time (vs. time-filling)?
- Are you enjoying your leisure activities or just spending time?
- How balanced is your leisure today?

Tom retired at age 59 from his job as an accountant and now spends much of his time at the golf course. Typically, he plays golf each weekday morning, taking Saturdays and Sundays off. "I guess I've just replaced my job with my golf," he said, laughing. "I get up during the week at the same time and head for the course. I play with the same guys, spend the same amount of time after the round at the nineteenth hole and get home at the same time. Golf now takes up most of my time during the week and I don't really have a lot of other interests."

On one hand, you might say that Tom's steady diet of golf is OK as long as he is happy. *Let's examine why Tom is happy:*

- He loves to golf and he can golf every day.
- He doesn't have any other interests and golf is a good way to pass the time.
- He doesn't like to stay at home.
- Golf is the only thing in his life that gives him satisfaction.

When you look at any leisure activity that you undertake, how does it make you feel? Could Tom do other things to balance out his time and make his leisure more special? There is no hard answer to this. We know from the research that successful retirees vary their leisure activities and use them to achieve happiness. However, if you were to ask Tom, he might reply, "If it isn't broken…don't fix it"

Are you doing the same with your leisure?

## Balancing Your Leisure In Retirement

Your Second Life opens the opportunity to redefine free time and reframe leisure to maximize life enjoyment. If you find a way to redefine work in positive rather than negative terms, you can begin to view work as another leisure activity.

*For most Americans, leisure time can be divided into six components:*

• **Social Interaction:** time spent with family, friends and others to share ideas, energy, support, etc.

• **Spectator Appreciation:** time spent passively watching others—e.g. attending sporting or artistic events, watching movies and television, etc.

• **Solitary Relaxation:** time spent thinking about your world and your place in it, including possibilities, dreams, and plans

• **Physical Activity:** time spent on enjoyable physical activities that maintain your wellness

• **Creative Expression:** time spent creating, writing, composing, expressing your ideas, etc.

• **Intellectual Stimulation:** time spent expanding your level of information, knowledge, understanding, skill

## Varying Your Retirement Leisure

Some leisure is just that—leisure. It's your retirement and you want to enjoy it as much as you can. There will be times when you choose to do nothing or to do what you want. That's OK, but consider the goals of your leisure activities and try to balance those also.

*Your leisure can have three main goals:*

• Pleasurable activities that you undertake purely for the joy of doing them
• Meaningful activities that create positive emotion and are tied to your values
• Engaging activities that involve other people and "flow" activities

## Your Leisure Activities Over Time

Continuity theory (Chapter 9) suggests that our leisure activities in our Second Lives will reflect our previous leisure activities. In other words, we generally don't do a lot of new things at this stage of life. This doesn't mean that you can't, just that most of us continue to live as we have always lived (and done what we have always done).

As we age, there is a tendency to use leisure to create emotionally meaningful activities that continue to make us feel good about growing older. Our leisure activities increasingly define our view of how relevant we feel, our social network and ourselves. As a result, for many of us, leisure gains importance with age.

Research suggests that our social contacts and leisure become intertwined with aging; many of us will eliminate social relationships that do not contribute to satisfying leisure activities (Baltes, 1990).

Your challenge at this phase of life is to push yourself to do new things and go new places. However, simply wishing for these things doesn't automatically make them happen.

## What Will You Do With This Information?

## Exercise

### How Balanced Is Your Leisure?

The self-assessment below will give you a snapshot of how you currently take advantage of your leisure time.  How do you spend your leisure time today? Tick off those activities that you expect to do more of in your Second Life.

| SOCIAL INTERACTION | SPECTATOR APPRECIATION |
|---|---|
|  |  |

| SOLITARY CONTEMPLATION | PHYSICAL ACTIVITY |
| --- | --- |
| | |
| CREATIVE EXPRESSION | INTELLECTUAL STIMULATION |
| | |

## What did you learn?

How balanced is your leisure today? Are there some activity areas that have "gotten away" from you and that you just don't spend a lot of time in? What do you want to change in this next phase of your life?

*The best test of our intelligence is how we spend our leisure.*

**—Dr. Laurence Peter**

### DID YOU KNOW?

• Americans aged 55-64 are the fastest-growing number of users of information technology

• Some 82% of boomers use the Internet and 64% are online. Their online activities include instant messaging, downloading music or movies, financial transactions and online gaming.

# CHAPTER 22
## Travel and Retirement

### SOME THINGS TO CONSIDER:
• What are some of the issues with travel that you should be aware of?
• What kind of travel will be the best for you?
• How much does it cost?
• How does travel change over time?

In a recent study of Americans' travel expectations for retirement, 71% considered travel in retirement an important goal worth saving for; 47% regarded it not as a luxury but a necessity. Still, only 15% placed a high priority on saving for travel, even though as a retirement priority it ranks second only to spending more time with family and friends.

Travel is one of those "expected" retirement activities that most people dream about. You now have time to go to all of those places that you always wanted to visit. Europe? No problem. A motorbike trip across the country? Let's get going!

Travel has many health benefits in addition to providing you with the opportunity to visit new places and change your routine. As the old saying goes, "A change is as good as a rest." Not all travel is stress-free or restful. However, its positive health benefits stem from the happiness and engagement created with family and friends, fun activities and peaceful meditation.

### Some Travel Issues To Think About

Before you decide that your entire retirement is going to be about travel, here are some things to consider:

• Incorporate the annual cost of travel as a fixed cost into your yearly retirement budget.

• Don't think of travel as a strictly leisure activity, but consider its health benefits as well.

• You can travel with family and friends, and combine your retirement goals into your trips.

• Remember that travel does not have to be exotic or expensive to have health, family and social benefits.

• Don't just travel for the sake of travel. Some people are not happy with where they are and feel that changing scenery will change them. This doesn't usually work.

## Paying For Travel

One approach taken by retirees is to set up a pool of money to pay for their trips each year. The rule of thumb for a 3% inflation rate and 30 years of withdrawals is to multiply the amount you are taking out each year by 20. For example, if you plan to spend $10,000 per year on travel you can create an account of $200,000 over and above what you need to live comfortably and spend out of that account.

Domestic travel inflation rates have basically matched inflation over the past three decades. However, international travel is one of those retirement issues that will likely carry a higher inflation rate than other living expenses. For example, in Canada the TPI (Travel Price Index) has been roughly 0.25% higher than the Consumer Price Index since 2005. Airline fares have gone up by a third in that time, and the expectation is that this gap will widen further in the future.

Normally, you aren't trying to pay for 30 years of travel. If your retirement plans begin at age 65, you may be looking at 20 years of travel. Also, this travel is not likely to be international each year but a mixture of some international and some domestic.

## Using Travel To Stretch Your Retirement Dollars

There are places in the world that are far less expensive to live than in the U.S. If you have a sense of adventure, you might look at places such as Costa Rica, Panama, Malaysia, Mexico and Thailand as alternatives. The best advice is to "practice retirement" there first to see if you like the lifestyle.

It is not green grass and palm trees that will determine how happy you will be, but the strength of your social network. Successful travellers will build a new social network where they relocate, while those who do not will likely report that they are as miserable as they were when they lived in snow up north.

## Snowbird Travel

Bill and Dianne retired five years ago and purchased a home in Sun City Grande just outside of Phoenix, Ariz. Typically, they travel south around the first of November and stay to the end of April. "We bought at the right time," said Bill. "Prices had fallen significantly throughout the southern U.S. in the midst of the credit crisis and we were able to get a nice house that fit our retirement needs." Dianne said that the couple "loves the lifestyle and the fact that we can just get in our golf cart and drive to the golf course. There are social programs on all of the time and we have developed a great set of friends who do the same thing every year."

If you don't want to move full-time to another locale, you may want to consider the snowbird lifestyle. Many Americans flock to Florida, Arizona, California and other southern climes each winter to take advantage of warm weather and a leisurely lifestyle. There are many communities acorss the southern U.S. that have sprouted, providing social opportunities and a retirement lifestyle.  Many have golf courses, tennis courts, pools etc. Most resort locations will offer golf discounts for residents.

## How Travel Can Change Over Time

Generally, your travel patterns will change over time. As you age, you will often move toward less stressful travel and to family travel. Your "heavy" trips will most often come in the first few years of your retirement, but that doesn't mean to say that you won't have these adventures in later life!

## What Did You Learn?

# CHAPTER 23
## Creating Your Bucket List

**SOME THINGS TO CONSIDER:**

• Are you the kind of person who likes to set goals and then achieve them?

• Are there places that you want to visit or things you want to accomplish in your life?

• Does everyone really need a bucket list?

*I don't want to get to the end of my life and find that I lived just the length of it. I want to have lived the width of it as well.*

— **Diane Ackerman**, *author, poet and naturalist*

At one of our retirement workshops, I met a woman named Janet. She was in her early 70s and was a bundle of energy. She told me that she had 15 things on her bucket list and that every time she achieved one of her goals, she crossed it off and added a new goal. While she was focused on finishing each goal, her real ambition was to die with 15 new things on her list.

The first known use of the term bucket list in popular culture only dates back to 2006. In 2007, a popular movie starring Jack Nicholson brought the term to prominence. Simply put, a bucket list is all of the things that you want to do "before you kick the bucket."

## Why Draw Up A Bucket List?

"I don't need a bucket list," said a 55-year-old lawyer when I asked my audience who among them had a written bucket list. "Whenever I want to do something, I just go ahead and do it," he said somewhat dismissively. "Bucket lists are for those people who have to dream."

Clearly, he was determined to let me know that he already had success in life and that one of the advantages of being successful is that you don't have to create goals anymore.

Granted, not everyone thinks like that; if you only look at a bucket list as a way to live your dreams and live your values, there are many people who are already living their dreams as they enter retirement.

A bucket list can be a set of goals that you would like to achieve. The list is a structure that focuses you on the strategy needed to achieve those goals and a way of measuring whether you have been successful or not.

The idea of the bucket list will be different for everyone. It is, after all, dependent on whether you like to set goals, whether you strive to accomplish things and if you like to dream about things in your future.

It will also look a lot different if you differentiate between using your bucket list to simply achieve a goal or to explore the values that drive your retirement life.

## The Difference Between A Value And A Goal

Our lawyer friend sees the need to set goals as superfluous; he'd already achieved what he wanted to and felt no need to continue. The bigger issue, though, is what's left? What can he do to continue to challenge himself, to create positive energy, to live rather than just do what he has always been doing?

The answer: think of a bucket list as reinforcing your values rather than simply achieving a goal. If you have always wanted to see New York, getting there is a goal. However, if it is important to you to travel and explore the world as part of the values you hold, your trip to New York is a reinforcement of that.

In Chapter 2, we looked at the importance of the values that you have and that will be the foundation of your Second Life. Your values are powerful drivers for your sense of achievement; in fact, when Maslow talked about "self-actualization," he was really talking about living your life based on achieving the values you have.

Let's look at the advantage of setting values-based goals from a psychological perspective and establish that you are more likely to do something if it is part of a goal strategy that you have set.

## Goal-Setting And Achievement

In Chapter 8, we looked at the role that achievement plays in retirement;

in fact, it was one of the five keys to retirement happiness in the PERMA model. Achieving bucket-list goals is a good way to replace goal-setting and achievement that would normally come from the workplace.

## How To Build Values-Based Goals

Earlier, we had you look at your key values that would guide you through your next phase of life. Here is a strategy to form goals for retirement that could fill your bucket list and fit the values that you hold.

1. List the most important values that you have.

2. Identify activities that would allow you to engage in the values you have.

3. Look at the areas of your life where these values might apply and then see how many areas you could create goals for each value.

- Health
- Personal
- Work
- Spiritual
- Family
- Relationships
- Leisure
- Community

## Different Kinds Of Bucket Lists

There are, of course, more kinds of bucket lists than the values-based list we looked at above. *A bucket list is also a way to:*

- Organize your goals and create the strategies to reach them

- Push yourself to identify other new things that you can do

- Provide a way for you to "keep score" and build achievement in retirement

Most would think that a bucket list is just a travel goal. It can go much further than that. *A bucket list can include:*

✔ The intellectual achievements you want to attain

✔ Social achievements that focus on nurturing and supporting your social network

✔ Personal goals that help you grow spiritually

✔ Creative goals that focus on your creativity and help you rediscover your passions

- ✓ Physical goals that promote health and wellness

- ✓ Spectator goals that allow you to see things you have never seen before

## Creating 'Smart' Goals

Now that you have a values-based bucket list that you have prioritized, let's focus on the "urgent" values and goals on your list and create some "smart" goals. Smart goal-setting is something that we have all done in the workplace, but few of us actually take the same approach in our personal lives.

In retirement, there is a big difference between wishes and goals—the two are not the same. A goal has a strategy attached to it. In fact, research suggests that you are more likely to achieve a goal if you have a strategy than if you don't. In fact, psychologist Henry Locke's research on goal-setting found that you could increase the chances of achieving a goal by 90% if the goal is specific and challenging.

Many of the same tools and techniques we developed to support our personal growth in our working career can serve us well in retirement.

A bucket list can be a challenging goal. It is the "specific" part that turns a wish such as "I want to visit Italy" into a goal. Where specifically do you want to go? Will that make the goal successful? Is going to Rome achievable? Is this a realistic goal today given your circumstances, or would it be more realistic tomorrow? What kind of time frame should you put on it?

When you answer these questions, you are taking the SMART goal approach. *Here are its elements:*

**S**pecific: Your goals have to be as specific as possible to make them real. In fact, the more detail that you can put into your goal, the better chance you have to achieve it.

**M**easurable: You want to ensure that your retirement goals can be quantified. Remember that old question: "If you don't know where you are going, how will you know when you get there?"

**A**chievable: It is great to have a goal, but is it achievable given your situation? Personally, I would like to run a marathon; I am 60 years old and have bad knees. Does that eliminate the goal? (Probably not—I will figure it out!)

**R** **ealistic:** Is the goal realistic today or sometime in the future? Would the time that you take be better spent on something else? Would your goal create conflict with someone you love? In my case, the goal isn't realistic until I get my knees looked at!

**T** **ime-bound:** What kind of time frame are you looking at? If you think that you could complete your goal in three years, put that date down. If you find later that this goal won't work, don't discard the goal, just change the time frame.

## Exercise

### Your Key Values That Will Drive Your Fulfilling Activities
*(look back at Chapter 2 if you have forgotten)*
*In the middle column, prioritize your values.*

| Your Value | | Some specific goals in areas of your life such as: health, personal, work, spiritual, family, relationships and leisure |
|---|---|---|
| 1. | | |
| 2. | | |
| 3. | | |
| 4. | | |
| 5. | | |
| 6. | | |
| 7. | | |
| 8. | | |

Now ask yourself, which one of these values is the strongest? Prioritize your values in terms of which one means the most to you in your Second Life. Then, list some of the goals that you might have in each of these areas (if they apply). Note that "money" is not a life area in this discussion but can be applied to each area.

As you look at the above list of values and the goals that relate to each, think about which goals are "urgent" versus those goals that could be "left to later." Any goal that is directly related to the most important value that you hold is probably an urgent goal. Others, based on those values that have lower priority in your life, could be left to another time.

# Exercise

## Your Bucket List By Type Of Activities

In the exercise below, think of some things that you have always wanted to accomplish. Make sure that these goals fit the SMART formula we talked about above. Try to fit several goals in the categories below.

| SOCIAL GOALS | SPECTATOR GOALS |
|---|---|
|  |  |
| SPIRITUAL GOALS | PHYSICAL GOALS |
|  |  |

| CREATIVE GOALS | INTELLECTUAL GOALS |
|---|---|
| | |

| SPIRITUAL GOALS | PHYSICAL GOALS |
|---|---|
| | |

# CHAPTER 24
## Your Retirement Home Is Your Castle

### SOME THINGS TO CONSIDER

• Does your current home meet your needs in retirement?

• What changes would you make to where you live?

• What would have to happen for you to consider a change to where you live?

• Have you thought about where you will live if you can no longer look after yourself?

We wrote this chapter because we often see retirees living in homes that no longer meet their needs but who refuse to consider a change. We will establish that a home should never be a source of distress for you and that it should continue to reflect the life you wish to live. The problem is that the emotional attachment we have to our homes may cloud our ability to make a rational decision.

Richard and Marielle retired five years ago from their jobs in Seattle  Both had enjoyed successful careers, raised three children and lived an upscale lifestyle that included a large home in one of the better neighbourhoods in their city.

When they retired, the couple continued to live in their home. "We still had two teenagers that we had to support and we were convinced that our oldest was going to come back home," said Marielle. "We could not conceive of selling a house that we loved, at least while our children might still need us."

However, in the past five years, Richard and Marielle have become "empty nesters. All of a sudden, the home that they so dearly loved became more of a burden than it did a source of comfort and pride.

"We found that we were travelling far more than we thought we would," noted Richard. "That means that we end up worrying about the house, about watering the plants and shovelling the walks while we are away. Besides, why would we need such a big house when our lifestyle had seen us try to simplify as many things as possible in our day-to-day lives?"

Recently, Richard and Marielle made the decision to sell the family home and to buy a condo on Lake Union. They held a big garage sale, which forced them to part with many prized possessions that they could no longer place in their new home. "It was time to shift gears," said Marielle. "This was a new life for us and we both had to make an effort to move on."

## Home Is Where The Heart Is

We had previously talked about continuity theory. It says that "you are who you are" and that as you get older you tend to become even more so. When it comes to your home, there is a tendency to view where you live in emotional rather than utilitarian terms. For many Americans, taking a rational view of how well their homes will suit them in retirement is very difficult.

It is often said that your home is a reflection of who you are. If you have lived there for any length of time, it is also a storehouse for your memories. This is where your children grew up, where important family events took place. It has become part of you emotionally.

## Is Your Home Your Retirement Plan?

American boomers have been the beneficiaries of the housing boom that occurred from 1996 to 2007. However, home ownership for the over-55 cohort has been falling; this has been blamed in part on higher divorce rates, as well as the trend by pre-retiring boomers to use money for lifestyle or retirement rather than paying down their mortgages.

The concern for the future is that there will also be many American boomers who will enter retirement either carrying a mortgage or having little equity in their homes. According to BMO/Harris Bank, close to 60% of retiring Americans expect to carry a mortgage into retirement. This will require them to spend higher amounts on their living arrangements, as more will become renters rather than owners.

A large number of Americans expect to use the equity in their homes to fund their retirement. the AARP suggests that nearly a quarter of Americans expect their homes to be their primary source of income when they leave the workforce and that as many as 35% to 40% of Americans may rely on their homes to fund retirement.

## Does Your Home Meet Your Needs?

Many people on the verge of retirement will say that they are living in the same home they will live in throughout their retirement. While that makes sense today, will it make sense in the future?

If you look dispassionately at your home, would it still meet your needs in five years? What about 10 years and beyond? *Here are some things to consider:*

- Ease and cost of maintenance
- Need for housekeeper, gardener, etc.
- Cost of heat, power, air conditioner, etc.
- Presence of stairs
- Handicap accessibility
- Proximity to social network
- Climate
- Proximity to health-care facilities
- Security
- Need for renovation
- Real estate market
- Access to recreation facilities
- Internet connection

## Should You Downsize Or Move?

Where you live is certainly your choice, but the key determinant factor is whether this new home fits your retirement lifestyle. The list above is a good one to use in assessing the suitability of a new home as an alternative to where you currently live.

Our advice is not to make a quick decision on moving soon after retirement. Give things time to settle and give yourself a chance to sample retirement life to decide what you really want.

Downsizing makes good sense for some people because it can be a financially sound and less stressful alternative to where you live now.

Downsizing also gives you more control over your life; you may no longer have space for adult children to move back or room to deal with a steady stream of visitors at your new beach home!

If you have decided that you want to move, make that decision well in advance of retirement and then create the plans to make it happen on your time schedule. You also may want to "practise retirement" in your chosen place first if you intend to move to a new community. Pretend you are retired and use your vacation time to spend some time there.

"Let's see... Deer and antelope playing, no discouraging words, and no cloudy skies. I've got just the place!"

## Retirement Communities

A popular trend for American retirees is moving to a retirement community, in US or elsewhere. Some of these communities have tremendous social programs that will help you stay active and interact with new friends. Considering what we have discussed earlier in this book about the need for a social network and meaningful, engaging activities, there is a lot to be said for this lifestyle.

Not everyone is comfortable with the close proximity to others or the feeling that you have sacrificed your independence. Others may feel that if they move into one of these communities they are throwing in the towel and admitting they are "old."

While most villages are designed for 55-plus retirees, the average age of most communities is often considerably older, so you should check this out first to see if it works for you.

## Things to check:

- ✔ Conformity rules that may limit some freedom to do what you want in "your" place (satellite dishes, outdoor heaters, ornaments, etc.)
- ✔ Security within the complex
- ✔ Homeowner association fees
- ✔ Maintenance quality for common areas, pools, etc.
- ✔ Policy regarding overnight guests, grandchildren, etc.
- ✔ Parking for visitors
- ✔ Clubhouse rental
- ✔ Access to recreational facilities (gyms, golf, pools)

## What About A Vacation Home?

There are advantages and disadvantages to a vacation home in another part of the province or country. The advantage is that you can significantly cut down on vacation costs if you vacation at the country home instead. However, the disadvantage is that you may feel committed to going to your second home and miss some opportunities to go elsewhere. Also, a vacation home can significantly affect your annual budget.

Holiday destinations are attractive places to move in retirement, but remember that your experience with the location may have been on a shorter vacation. If you are going to live there permanently, you should "practice retirement" first to ensure that the community offers you everything that you want. Some downsides to holiday destinations are lots of visitors (some you want and some you don't), lots of tourists and higher prices.

A bigger issue is that the vacation home may be the dream of one person in the couple, while the partner goes along with the idea without really being enthusiastic. This can be overcome by making sure that you are both on the same page about what you both want. Think about taxes, insurance, maintenance, capital gains and estate planning issues.

## Making Your Own Home Ready For Your Second Life

Now that you are moving into this next phase of life, you should take the opportunity to look at everything about your current home with fresh eyes. Remember that you are trying to take all of the stress out of your life in retirement and there may be some things about your home that may become irritants later.

*Some examples are:*
• Home improvement issues that you never seem to get to
• Rooms that just don't work if you are both at home more
• A yard that requires more work than you are willing or able to keep up with
• A kitchen that is hard to work in efficiently
• Handicap requirements
• Guest rooms

If you are handy and can look at your home as a home improvement project, you can spend a lot of happy hours renovating. If this is not attractive to you, then you may have to pay someone else to do it. By the way, if you are a do-it-yourself individual, plan your projects ahead of time and try to avoid creating a constant state of construction in your home. That doesn't make for a stress-free or relaxing retirement!

## Clearing The Clutter

Have you noticed how much clutter accumulates in your home over a long period of time? It is natural to accumulate things, to the point where you no longer even look at them. For example, you have kept a lot of your old memories, children's toys, old photos and a lot of things that you just can't bring yourself to throw away. Take the time to go through everything, and find ways to catalogue what you want and to send the rest to a charity or give it away.

For example, old photos can be transferred to a digital format and old music to your iPad. Those old family movies can also be transferred to DVD.

In making your home work for you in your Second Life, it is a good idea to pick a day each year or each six months to go through your home and get rid of or file those things that are just taking up space. As a general rule of thumb, if you haven't looked at or used something in the past year you should think about getting rid of it. A garage sale is a great way to clear out things up that you no longer need, and generate some extra cash besides.

# Exercise

## Does Your Home Meet Your Retirement Needs?

In the exercise below, compare how big the major home issues are today versus how they might affect you in the future. If you feel that something might be an issue, simply put a check mark in the space that fits your expected time frame.

| Possible issue with your home today | What issues would you face from 5-10 years from now? | What issues might you face beyond 10 years? |
| --- | --- | --- |
| Ease and cost of maintenance | | |
| Need for housekeeper, gardener, etc. | | |
| Cost of heat, power, air conditioner, etc. | | |
| Presence of stairs | | |
| Handicap accessibility | | |
| Proximity to social network | | |
| Proximity to health-care facilities | | |
| Security | | |
| Climate | | |
| Need for renovation | | |
| Real estate market | | |
| Family move in/out | | |
| Change in relationship | | |
| Loss of spouse | | |
| Access to transportation | | |
| Access to international airport | | |
| Access to recreation | | |

Based on your review of these issues, what circumstances would cause you to change where you live?

## DID YOU KNOW?

• Those who are 55 and over are more likely to see proximity to family as the key factor in deciding on retirement location, compared with those 45–54.

• Those who are 65 years and older are the most likely to rate health-care facilities in the community as the principal consideration. Regardless of age, women are more likely than men to have considered proximity to family in planning for retirement, according to the BMO Retirement Institute.

• 61% of boomers plan to buy a detached house when they move from their current one. Four in five respondents want those homes to be smaller, but almost half of respondents want them to be more luxurious. Only 25% of boomers are considering condos for their next move.

# PART 7

"It seems rather late to be taking out a retirement pension. I suggest you start doing the lottery instead."

## YOUR MONEY AND YOUR LIFE

# CHAPTER 25

## Are You Financially Comfortable To Enjoy Your Second Life?

### SOME THINGS TO CONSIDER:

• Do you know how much money you will need to enjoy your retirement?

• Will the combination of Social Security, your 401K plan, your IRA and your savings be enough?

• Have you considered the length of time you may require money in retirement?

Recently, Mary visited her advisor to review her financial plan for retirement. Mary, 58, recently made the decision to retire from her advertising job and was looking forward to enjoying her retirement years. She became extremely troubled, however, as she prepared to meet with her advisor. It seemed that over the past year she had marked more "down" days in her portfolio than up days as she calculated the daily market value of her retirement nest egg, She began to worry at night that her retirement dreams would fall victim to some catastrophic event that would wipe out her assets. Mary's concern began to overshadow her life and worrying about her money became extremely stressful for her.

### Your Money In Retirement

In retirement, your money will take on a new role. Rather than saving and investing for the future, you now move to converting your wealth to income, protecting what you have and ultimately transferring it to other people or causes you care about.

Your financial health will play a very important role in your overall retirement happiness and it is valuable to think about how you view money, investing and your "financial comfort."

Throughout this book we have focused on the need to develop your ability to handle the changes you will face in your Second Life. The three major stressors that affect many people as they enter retirement are their health, their relationships and their financial security. And of these three, financial security is the one that many feel they have less knowledge about and less control over.

The vagaries of investment markets, the unexpected expenses that crop up when you least expect them and the barrage of information from advisors, books, advertisers and the media keep our financial affairs in the forefront of our consciousness.

Whether you have a great deal of it or believe that you don't have enough, money can be a source of stress. This may arise from the belief that money is a reflection of success or failure in life. In fact, having money is often confused with "being happy"— "the more money I have, the happier I will be."

In retirement, the pressure to have and keep what you have worked hard to accumulate may build. As you look at the things that you would like to do, the places that you want to visit and the opportunities that you want to take advantage of, you will likely pay close attention to the financial resources that you have available.

However, your financial situation does not need to be the source of stress or uncertainty. Instead, your financial health can serve as part of the foundation for building a meaningful and fulfilling Second Life.

## The Role That Money Plays In Your Second Life

From a psychological perspective, money takes on a different role when we consider its contribution to this next phase of our life. When we were accumulating money in our earlier life, it was a source of pride and a way to keep score of our growing success in earning and saving.

As you transition into your Second Life, the future has arrived. Now, as you look at the monies you have put aside in your nest egg, there is a different emotional impact. In fact, money is a means to an end rather than the end in itself! Consider how it might affect you emotionally:

**1. Money equals security.** This is your ability to sleep at night and to know that regardless what happens, you are going to be all right.

**2. Money dictates lifestyle**. Your spending tends to reflect the income you have. In retirement, your ability to do some of the things that you want to do is tied to whether you can afford it.

**3. Money provides independence.** As you get older, independence becomes more of a challenge and a goal. Your financial resources can dictate how much independence you really have.

**4. Money helps family.** Whether it is your ability to help a family member in need, provide caregiving for a spouse or distribute your assets as part of your estate, your money will dictate whether you can be there for your family.

**5. Money creates a legacy.** When you think about the causes that are important to you, the community you wish to help or the legacy you wish to leave your family, the strength of your financial resources will determine the legacy you create.

## Defining 'Financial Comfort' In Retirement

We define financial comfort as living with a financial situation that does not cause you undue stress on a daily basis! *This means:*

• You can do the things you want to do given the lifestyle you have created.
• You can handle unexpected challenges to your financial situation.
• You spend your money in a way that is congruent with your core values.

Most people work to achieve an income that will allow them to be financially comfortable. However, there isn't one definition of financial comfort; it means different things to different people. And while many people can easily identify what being uncomfortable financially means to them, they have not really clarified what they mean by "financial comfort."

The list below outlines several financial situations. As you think about your current situation, identify which of the items listed would make you uncomfortable today:

☐     Your mutual fund portfolio is down 25% over the past year and the newspapers are full of talk about a "stock market meltdown."

☐     Interest rates continue to fall and the money that you have in guaranteed investments pays you less each month.

☐ A newspaper article that you read suggests that health care, nursing costs and prescription drug costs will continue to rise and that insurance coverage will continue to decline over time.

☐ There has been talk around your workplace about early layoffs and there have been some suggestions that your current job may be eliminated before you actually get a chance to retire.

As you look at each of these situations, think about the ramifications for your current financial situation. What kind of emotional reaction do you have? Think about how this reaction affects your current retirement plan. What kind of emotional reaction do you have when you think about how this affects your retirement planning today?

## Now, Imagine That You're 10 Years Older

You are that much closer to the next stage in your life or you have already transitioned into your retirement years. Does your definition of financial comfort change as you think about your future? Looking at the list again, identify which financial matters would make you uncomfortable as you begin your Second Life:

As you review each of these situations, what kind of emotional reactions do you think you will have 10 years from now when you think about the ramifications for your retirement plans?

Depending on your circumstances, you might not have any concerns about the above situations. For example, you may not be particularly concerned about the ups and downs of the stock market, but instead recognize that these ebbs and flows are normal. You might have insurance coverage that would protect you from rising health-care costs. You might not care that you can't travel the world every year and that you may have to take a trip every five years instead of yearly. Finally, you may have put a plan into place that allows you to leave your present job and replace the income with money you have saved, or to earn income from a new career opportunity that you looked into earlier.

The key to financial comfort isn't how much money you have, it is how you feel about your financial situation. And what impacts how you feel about your financial situation is your definition of financial security, how that definition translates into what you want your money to do for you, how much control you feel you have over your financial situation, and how much you know about making your money work for you.

My grandmother used to advise that we should "cut our coat by our cloth." In her Scottish wisdom, she let me know that I should never live beyond my means. In retirement, this also means making adjustments to lifestyle so that a reversal in the stock market is not likely to change the way you live.

## What Will You Do With This Information?

### DID YOU KNOW?

• Collectively boomers are the wealthiest generation in history, but only 10% are truly affluent. Only 35% of American baby boomers are debt-free. More than 50% of American boomers are still paying off mortgages.

# CHAPTER 26
## *Five Keys to Achieving Financial Comfort*

### SOME THINGS TO CONSIDER:
• How much do you know about managing your financial affairs today?

• What do you remember about your earliest lessons about money?

• How many of your habits today reflect what you learned in the past?

• How will you view your money in retirement?

Bert and Marlene, a professional couple who retired on Bert's 50th birthday, had never prepared a budget when they were working. Bert related, "We had no children and we were leading a life with lots of income. We never thought about what we wanted to do with our money or how we were spending it. If we needed to make a purchase or pay a bill, we would write a cheque. However, when we retired we recognized that our financial advisors had taught us how to save money, but no one ever taught us how to spend money.

"For the first two years of our retirement, we started to keep track of everything that we were spending. Our friends thought we were being unnecessarily analytical, but we really wanted to get a handle on where our money was going."

Marlene added, "Now we have a really good idea of what our life costs, which allows us to plan ahead for our trips and those things we consider to be our retirement extravagances. If we didn't know how much we were working with, we would be spending blindly, and neither one of us is willing to do that anymore!"

Before considering specifics surrounding any financial strategies during retirement, it is important to ensure we have **a solid understanding of money**, and it shapes are decision making. There are five keys to understanding money and it's role in providing financial comfort in your Second Life.

### ☞ Key #1: Ongoing Education on Financial Matters

We all know the expression, "Knowledge is power" although a more accurate phrase might be "Applied knowledge is power." In other words, the goal is to use your general knowledge of financial matters to enable you to view your financial situation as objectively as possible. Ideally, your knowledge of financial matters should protect you from stress and irrational fears as you view your financial situation.

Part of this knowledge includes having a *general* idea of what investment options are open to you, the tax considerations on your retirement nest egg and a basic understanding of investment markets with an awareness of where interest rates are headed. We are not suggesting you need to become a financial expert, especially with the scores of experts available to help with the details of investment strategies, tax planning, estate planning and a myriad of other considerations.

Some of you enjoy following the markets, with some even turning financial knowledge into a hobby. Or you may rely on regular contact with your financial advisor to keep you up to date on financial matters, ensuring that you view your financial situation objectively. It all depends on your personal style. The key to education on financial matters is to understand enough so that the issue of money is less stressful in your Second Life.

According to a 2013 Sun Financial study, 56% of men surveyed felt confident about their understanding of financial issues needed to make a retirement plan, versus 47% of women.

Jim, 60, is a retired geologist living in Halifax. He has always been interested in his investments and has handled his own portfolio for a number of years. The introduction of online trading meant that Jim no longer had to deal with an investment advisor and was able to use his own information and research to buy and sell stocks. Jim's routine each day in his retirement is to catch the stock market opening at 6:30 a.m. on his computer. Jim stays at his desk until 10 a.m. or 11 a.m. each morning, reading information, watching two business networks on his two television sets, and trading his portfolio. When asked how he was enjoying his retirement, he said, "I am not retired. I have become a professional investor."

### ☞ Key #2: 'The Meaning of Money'

Ron S. : "I grew up in a household where my parents didn't have the money they needed to live the lifestyle that they chose. My father believed that it was more important to look the part than to earn it. I still remember extravagant holidays and dinners out, followed by bill collectors and my parents fighting over money. I told myself that this would never happen to me, but I can't seem to save any money either. If it weren't for my wife, we would be completely broke."

For many, money is an emotional catalyst that can act as a stimulant or a depressant, depending on the day and the individual. Some people become so focused on their financial situation that it overshadows everything else in their lives. They live in fear that the money will not be there when they need it or that it will disappear, leaving them destitute. Others use money as a drug, spending it freely to make themselves feel better about who they are. Often, excessive spending can be the result of a self-image problem that is temporarily satiated by buying expensive toys, trips or meals.

Much of the meaning we attach to money and the role it plays in our lives comes to us from lessons we learned from our parents and others close to us during childhood. Understanding where your views on money came from and how they are linked to your stress level regarding money is important in maintaining your sense of financial comfort, now and in your Second Life.

When you look back, where do you think your views about money and its meaning in your life came from?

What attitudes and beliefs did your parents, grandparents, and others close to you in your childhood have about money?

Do you have a relationship with money that you feel need to be adjusted to be able live a Second Life in financial comfort?

### ⛓ Key #3: Financial Efficiency

Brian and Janet are affluent professionals who have begun to plan seriously for their retirement. One of the questions they asked during our workshop was, "How much is retirement actually going to cost?" They felt that they had done all of the right things financially to live the kind of life that they wanted, although they had no idea what their spending would look like in their Second Life. Janet had been told that most people spend less in retirement. "I can't believe that," she told me. "If Brian and I are going to do all of the things that we want to do, it's going to take a lot of money." I asked them if they could tell me how much money they spend today on their normal household budget. Brian laughed and said, "We talk all the time about creating a budget for ourselves, but the fact is that we never think about the money we spend or where it goes. We have always paid our bills and haven't had to worry."

Financial efficiency means knowing where you spend your money and allocating your resources to maximize it and increase the likelihood that you will have enough money to live the life you want.

Many people feel that budgeting is only for those who have limited resources. On the contrary, budgeting in your retirement makes sense regardless of how much money you have. A major source of stress and uncertainty in retirement can come from not having control of certain aspects of your financial situation. For example, your income may fluctuate if you are self-employed or receive income from your investments. Your expenditures may fluctuate if you are hit with unexpected bills that you hadn't counted on (health-care costs are a good example).

Keeping close tabs on revenues and expenditures can give you a sense of control, and therefore minimize your uncertainty and stress. If you find that managing your expenses and revenues is an activity you don't enjoy, perhaps you can ask a professional or a trusted friend who enjoys working with details to help get you started.

### ⌒ Key #4: Financial Efficacy

Belinda and Thomas had always been diligent about adding to their retirement nest egg. On the eve of their retirement they sat down with their financial advisor to make adjustments to their plan. They had talked about their day-to-day obligations in this new life and had a pretty good idea of where they wanted to spend their money. Their financial advisor asked how they felt about expenditures such as gifts, charitable contributions or other investments in their community. Belinda explained that they had never considered these things because they didn't feel that they had enough money to become philanthropic. "Our advisor pushed us to talk about how much we enjoyed contributing to our church and helping out our granddaughter," said Thomas. "He asked whether we were using any of our money to do things that we felt good about, things that were true to our values. I guess that we never really thought about it in that way."

Efficacy is your ability to use your money and other assets in a way that is in keeping with your values. Efficacy represents how effective you are in using your money to benefit the causes, charities and people you care deeply about. In Chapter 8 we discussed identifying your core values. What part of your retirement nest egg can you use in ways that are more consistent with your values?

Part of financial comfort is the knowledge that you are using your capital in a way that moves beyond simply looking after your normal living expenses to using your money in ways that promote your core values.

### ⚷ Key #5: Equilibrium

The last element of financial comfort is your personal assessment of the first four elements: education, meaning, efficiency and efficacy. Equilibrium means that you have balanced all four elements in your financial planning so that your money and other financial assets equal a comfortable positive versus an uncomfortable stressor in retirement.

The goal is to maximize the amount of enjoyment you gain from your money. Some of our workshop attendees (along with many financial services clients and their advisors) have become so caught up in understanding the nuances of markets, investment and tax strategies and asset allocation that they forget the critical idea that says, "It is not what money is, but what money *does* that matters."

How would you rate your equilibrium in balancing your level of financial education, meaning, efficiency and efficacy? Do you feel comfortable that you are planning, or have a plan, to maximize your personal sense of comfort, purpose and satisfaction in your Second Life?

In the next chapter, we will examine some day-to-day things that you can do in each area to increase your overall comfort about your money.

## Exercise

### My Parents, Grandparents Or Guardians Had The Following Attitudes And Beliefs About Money

| | | |
|---|---|---|
| ☐ Spendthrift | ☐ Value-conscious | ☐ Affluent |
| ☐ Savers | ☐ Insightful | ☐ Rational |
| ☐ Shoppers | ☐ Price-conscious | ☐ Generous |
| ☐ Extravagant | ☐ Risk-averse | ☐ Impoverished |
| ☐ Teachers | ☐ Optimistic | ☐ Sharing |
| ☐ Bargain hunters | ☐ Worried | ☐ Businesslike |
| ☐ Controlled | ☐ Risk takers | ☐ Middle class |
| ☐ Charitable | ☐ Pessimistic | ☐ Selfish |
| ☐ Conventional | ☐ Indebted | ☐ Cash payment |
| ☐ Ambivalent | ☐ Investors | ☐ Live beyond means |
| ☐ Foolhardy | ☐ Irrational | ☐ Enterprising |
| ☐ Economical | ☐ Flashy | ☐ Credit |

# Exercise

## Assessing Your Financial Efficiency

How efficient are you with your money? In other words, do you know where your money is going so that you can be sure that you are maximizing its use? Do you feel confident that you have enough to live the life you want?

For each of the statements below, assign yourself a score from 1 (least like me) to 5 (most like me). *The scoring key follows the exercise.*

| | |
|---|---|
| I keep a regular household budget that relates our income with our expenses and provides me with a clear financial picture each month. | 1 2 3 4 5 |
| I pay attention to the price of the items that I buy and try to look for the best combination of price and value. | 1 2 3 4 5 |
| When I reflect on money that I have drawn out of the bank, I have a reasonably good idea of where I spent it. | 1 2 3 4 5 |
| I will often sacrifice buying something if I am not certain where the money will come from in my budget. | 1 2 3 4 5 |
| I pay my credit cards off each month and use my cards as a cash-management device. | 1 2 3 4 5 |
| I try to "pay myself first" by putting a percentage of my income aside toward my long-term financial planning. | 1 2 3 4 5 |
| I keep my accounts up to date at all times and have a system in place that organizes my bill-paying activities. | 1 2 3 4 5 |
| I keep track of the money that I spend on my "extravagances" and will not spend if I don't feel that I can afford them. | 1 2 3 4 5 |
| My spouse or partner and I have a clear understanding of our day-to-day financial situation and have the same view on accounting for the money that we spend. | 1 2 3 4 5 |
| I make use of financial-planning or budgeting software to help me stay organized. | 1 2 3 4 5 |
| Total Score | |

*Scoring this exercise:*

**10-29:** You may not have the handle on your day-to-day financial affairs that you will need in your retirement. A wise person once said, "If you look after the pennies, the dollars look after themselves." Are you spending money as if there is an unlimited supply and not accounting for how you disperse it? In this next phase of your life, you will be faced with competing priorities for your money. It may be best to start deciding now what is important about each dollar you spend.

**30-39:** You may have some control over your expenditures but also might lack a structure that allows you to keep track. Financial comfort comes to many people if they know exactly what they spend. Keeping track doesn't mean you should spend less, or that you have to sacrifice. It means that you will have the data to make the right decisions for you—both short-term and long-term.

**40-50:** You seem to be in control of day-to-day expenditures and have created a system to help you manage your money. In your Second Life, this will serve you well as you work with more limited sources of income and competing demands.

## What Does This Say About You?

1. What does this tell you about the lessons that you learned about how to use your money?

2. Go back to the list above and check the attitudes you currently hold about money. Then, circle those attitudes about money that you share today with people who influenced you when you were growing up.

3. How happy are you with the current meaning that you have given money in your life? Are your core values reflected in the way you use your money? Are you using your money on activities that are aligned with your core values? Are you simply trying to "keep up with the Joneses"?

4. What obstacles have your habits with money placed on your ability to reach your life goals?

# Exercise

## What Do You Really Want Your Money To Do For You?

You want to be clear about what you believe your money should do for you today and in your Second Life. Review the list below and identify those things most important to you.

| I want enough money to… | This will improve my quality of life over the long run. | This is a short-term expense that provides me with fun. | This makes a contribution to other people and is true to my values. |
|---|---|---|---|
| Buy "toys" such as cars, vacation homes, electronics, etc. | | | |
| Save me from worry so that I don't have to be concerned about money | | | |
| Travel extensively on a regular basis so that I can see the world | | | |
| Educate myself by taking courses or degrees to improve my mind | | | |
| Buy a new home, downsize or move to a new location | | | |
| Play more, having the freedom to pursue leisure activities | | | |
| Get me out of debt so that I can start accumulating more money | | | |
| Protect me from the cost of illness so that my income will not be compromised | | | |
| Upgrade my lifestyle so that I can enjoy more of the finer things in life | | | |
| Gamble, speculate or use my money to generate more money and have fun doing it | | | |

| I want enough money to... cont'd | This will improve my quality of life over the long run. | This is a short-term expense that provides me with fun. | This makes a contribution to other people and is true to my values. |
| --- | --- | --- | --- |
| Give to my family | | | |
| Be philanthropic or help out the causes that I believe in | | | |
| Look after basic living expenses so that I am always secure that I have enough to live on | | | |
| Change my life by creating new opportunities to do or be something different | | | |
| Take a spiritual journey | | | |
| Invest for investing's sake so that I can make money management my main job | | | |
| Help pay for my children or grandchildren's education | | | |
| Look after my parents so that they can enjoy their later years | | | |
| Pay my bills so that I am not bothered by the arrival of the mail | | | |

Look at the things that you checked off. Do you see a pattern in the types of things you most want to spend money on? Are they material items? Short-term investments? Long-term investments? Or some combination of all of these? The goal is to have congruence between what you value and how you spend your money.

## Creating A Legacy

A new trend in financial planning is to create a legacy plan as opposed to an estate plan. Estate planning looks after the disposal of your assets in an efficient manner after you pass on, while legacy planning targets what you want your money to do while you are still alive, and the impact you want to make on society and/or on your family long after you pass on.

If you answer "yes" to several of the situations listed below, legacy planning may fit well for you.

| | |
|---|---|
| I keep an up-to-date will and have a clear idea of where I want my assets to pass to. | YES/NO |
| I get a great deal of satisfaction from giving to others or making contributions to charities, my community, etc. | YES/NO |
| I like to set aside a portion of my income on a regular basis to help others. | YES/NO |
| I have others whom I care about who could use some additional financial assistance to make their lives better. | YES/NO |
| I have some causes that I would like to contribute to on a regular basis. | YES/NO |
| I would like to free up some of my time to volunteer for charitable organizations. | YES/NO |
| I have made myself aware of potential tax benefits of charitable giving and have discussed these with my financial advisor. | YES/NO |

# Exercise

## What Is Your Level Of Financial Comfort Based On Your Knowledge Of Money?

For each of the statements below, assign yourself a score from 1 (least like me) to 5 (most like me). *The scoring key follows the exercise.*

| | |
|---|---|
| I have a basic understanding of the various kinds of investments that are available to me. | 1  2  3  4  5 |
| I am aware of the basic tax considerations on the various kinds of investments. | 1  2  3  4  5 |
| I have a good understanding of the way investment markets work, including the cycles that markets seem to follow. | 1  2  3  4  5 |
| I regularly read the business section of the newspaper or keep up by listening to the business reports on radio or TV. | 1  2  3  4  5 |

| | |
|---|---|
| I try not to get too caught up in the day-to-day changes that might affect my long-term investments. | 1  2  3  4  5 |
| I receive information and advice at least twice a year from a knowledgeable financial professional. | 1  2  3  4  5 |
| I know where all of my financial papers are and have them organized so that I can access information easily. | 1  2  3  4  5 |
| I have a basic understanding of the need to have a will and to organize my estate efficiently. | 1  2  3  4  5 |
| I try to attend seminars or workshops that will add to my knowledge of financial-planning issues. | 1  2  3  4  5 |
| I feel that I have enough knowledge of my financial affairs to make an informed decision, either on my own or with the help of a financial professional. | 1  2  3  4  5 |
| I try to "pay myself first" by putting a percentage of my income aside toward my long-term financial planning. | 1  2  3  4  5 |
| **Total Score** | |

## Scoring This Exercise:

*If you scored:*

**10-19:** You have chosen not to get involved in the basics of managing your money and learning how to use it. You may be missing many opportunities to make your money work for you. Even if you have a professional who can make decisions for you, your low level of knowledge may make it difficult for you to feel comfortable with things that you don't understand or to feel confident regarding decisions you have made on the advice of your financial advisor.

While not caring about money or financial affairs may appear to decrease your stress, the fact is that an understanding of day-to-day money issues is crucial to your financial comfort. Things such as budgeting, paying for a vacation or moving money to another financial institution all require a general knowledge of finance.

**20-29:** You may want to increase your basic knowledge of financial and investment affairs in order to get a better understanding of your money. The problem with not having enough knowledge is that it is difficult to make informed decisions or to feel comfortable about recommendations that are made to you by others. When something happens that you may not understand (falling stock markets, for example), you may become unnecessarily stressed.

**30-39:** You have a general idea about financial issues, although your knowledge could be strengthened in certain areas. You will still require the advice and guidance of a financial professional to fill in the gaps in your knowledge, but you have learned enough to make financial planning and money in general less stressful in your life. If you fall into this category and you still find yourself stressed, you might want to identify the issues that concern you and then increase your knowledge in those areas.

**40-50:** You are obviously on top of your financial situation. You may make decisions for yourself without an advisor, or you may still seek out experts to help you. Possessing a lot of knowledge is a good thing as long as you are not a prisoner of the process. Is your interest in financial affairs enjoyable, or does it add to your overall stress? If you find that you have become involved in the management of your investment portfolio or financial affairs to the point where your involvement is negatively affecting your emotions or your relationships with others, you may want to step back or seek the help of a professional.

## What Will You Do With This Information?

### DID YOU KNOW?

• As people age, they are less likely to make reasoned decisions about their money. They are more likely to be influenced by their own past experiences or lessons around money based on the example of people who influenced them. (Hammond et al., 1987; Kahneman, 1993)

# CHAPTER 27
## Creating a Financial Plan for the Future

### SOME THINGS TO CONSIDER:

• What do you expect to spend money on in retirement?
What unexpected things could happen that would change your plans?
• Have you considered how much you will spend each month in this next phase of life?
• How much does retirement really cost?
• How will your spending change over time?
• Do you have control over your spending?

*This chapter is not meant to be a comprehensive guide to financial planning in retirement.* Our goal is to identify the main financial planning issues you will face and provide you with a template to help you look at your money in relation to your retirement life.

"Just once I would like to have a discussion with my advisor that showed me that he really understood me!" Tom related. "While I don't expect him to be an expert on retirement, I would at least like to feel that he has put together a plan that fits my life."

Tom is on the verge of retirement from his job as a sales manager at a major manufacturing firm in St. Louis. Next year, he will be 60. Tom feels that he is now finally in a position to walk away from his job and start to enjoy life with his wife Margaret. They have been dreaming about their retirement and have already made plans to become snowbirds.

Tom's frustration comes from his financial advisor never having asked him about what he plans to do in the future. "All we ever talk about is money! I finally had to ask him if maybe Margaret should come into the office and sit down with him too," said Tom. "My advisor has never met my wife, even though we have a joint account."

This is not to say that Tom and Margaret's advisor hasn't done a good job for them in the 15 years that they have dealt with him. In fact, the advisor has made some good recommendations over time and has put them in reasonable financial shape on the eve of their retirement. Their retirement savings have continued to grow and, combined with pensions and Social Security should provide Tom and Margaret with a nice retirement income.

"Where we really need help now," said Margaret, "is in understanding just what we should be planning for in the future. Maybe that isn't what a financial advisor is supposed to do, but I don't know who else would be able to give us a heads-up on the financial considerations that we should plan for in retirement."

Like many Americans, Tom and Margaret are entering retirement without a clear understanding of this next phase of life. Intuitively, they recognize that their lives will change over time, but they are uncertain about how those changes will affect their financial plan or vice versa. They know however, that they will require a different kind of discussion with their advisor than simply setting a savings goal and then measuring against it on a regular basis.

"One of the things that I really don't know," said Tom, "is how much retirement is going to cost. My advisor said that we will have more than enough money so we really shouldn't worry, but I like to feel I have a handle on things."

Although Tom and Margaret can calculate how much they spend now, and then try to figure out how that will change over time, they are left with the feeling that a retirement financial plan has to start with their lifestyle issues first. It isn't just about numbers anymore if it is going to be relevant to their goals for the future.

"I guess that is where the disconnect comes with our advisor," said Margaret with a sigh. "I don't know how our advisor can possibly create a financial plan for our retirement without even asking us how we want to live it." What are some of your financial planning issues in retirement?

Many retirees (and their advisors0 believe that a retirement transition plan is just an investment strategy. Your retirement life will not be that simple! These are just a few of the issues you should consider as you develop a financial plan for retirement.

## Helping (And Protecting) Your Family

Family issues will drive many of the expenditures that you make in retirement. And some of your unexpected expenditures may come as a result of issues faced by the people you love. *Some things to think about are:*

- Helping parents
- Helping children and grandchildren
- Caregiving

ANDERSON

"Mom & Dad are my primary funding, but I get plenty of soft money from my grandparents."

## Enjoying (And Protecting) Your Lifestyle

Many of the things that you value about your retirement cost money! Your lifestyle will change over time and it is important to consider the kinds of lifestyle issues that may cause additional demands on your finances. *Some things to think about are:*

- Providing yourself with a "Paycheck for life"
- Protecting your family's lifestyle through effective use of insurance
- Having sufficient money to enjoy your changing lifestyle decisions
- Making your money grow to protect your lifestyle from inflation and taxes
- Budgeting and tracking where you spend your money

## Planning For The Expected And Unexpected

Retirement life will bring many changes over time. Much of your retirement planning will be to protect you and your partner, or to anticipate these changes and prepare yourself financially for them.
*Some issues to think about are:*

- Insuring against loss of your income

- Having money to pay for the unexpected issues that will appear in retirement

- Planning ahead to fund life needs such as health care expenses and ongoing caregiving

## Achieving A Level Of Financial Comfort

There are strategies that you can undertake to increase your comfort with where you are financially. Three of the biggest things you can do are: make yourself aware of where you are financially at all times; educate yourself on the basics of planning investing ; and getting high quality financial advice.
*Some of the things to think about are:*

- What would make you feel that you will be OK regardless of what happens in the stock market, the economy, etc.?

- What assets can you draw on if you need to? This should include home equity, your savings, inheritance, liquid assets, etc.

- What has to happen in the first 3-5 years of retirement for you to feel that you are "on track"? The next 3-5 years?

## Building A Legacy

Many people call this "estate planning" and it simply means preparing yourself to pass on your assets to the people or causes you care most about when you die. However, you can also create a "living legacy" and enjoy the satisfaction of helping others while you are still alive.
*Some things to think about are:*

- What is an equitable distribution of your assets to your heirs and the causes you are passionate about?

- What "legacy" goals do you have?

- Who or what would you enjoy seeing the benefits of your money while you are alive

## The Importance Of A Paycheck And A Budget

As you think about your income needs in retirement, an easy way to think about how you will "get paid" is to give yourself paychecks with the same frequency as when you were working. This is a great way to control your spending and help you budget.

It is a good idea to create a budget, even if you feel that you have more than enough money to live your retirement life without worry. A major mistake that many make is to stop paying attention to how they are spending money. Consider this, you spent the first half of your life filling up your personal "ATM." You will spend the second half of your life taking withdrawals. And we need to make we don't empty your "ATM" before you die.

**Here's how to create your retirement budget:**

**What you'll need:**
• Your last six to 12 months' worth of bank account statements
• Your last six to 12 months' worth of credit card statements
• Your last two pay stubs (and your spouse's if you are married)
• 6 to 8 coloured highlighters
• Last year's tax return

Use the information on the items above to see where your money has been going and use the highlighters to group expenses into categories. At the end of this chapter, we have included a sample retirement budget sheet; most major financial institutions have something similar on their websites.

Start by writing down the major categories of Essential and Discretionary or Enjoyment expenses. You can use the categories in the sample budget or name your own. However you do it, avoid creating too many categories as it will be difficult to track and will be difficult to really provide meaningful data. Also avoid too few categories as the information will be too generalized to be of much use. You want something simple and easy to use and track that is separated by Essential vs. Enjoyment.

## Your Planning Issues In Retirement

As you think about your planning issues, our suggestion is to move beyond things such as investment management, tax planning and income planning. A more effective way to think about your money in retirement is to start with the emotional issues that will affect the plan.

# What can we help you address?

| Helping and Protecting Family | Helping Children | Assisting Parents | Enjoying Lifestyle | Education | Health issues |
| Protecting and Enjoying Lifestyle | Replace Income | Family Security | Personal Health | Long-Term Care | Protecting Business |
| Achieving Financial Comfort | Building and Protecting Nest egg | Regular Paycheck | Pay Less Tax | Saving for Future | Freedom and Independence |
| Planning for the Future | Clarifying Vision | Health Challenges | Managing Change | Home | Lifestyle Enjoyment |
| Building a Legacy | Wills and Instructions | Preserve legacy | Directing legacy | Giving to Charity | Living Legacy |

## How Much Does Retirement Cost?

There is strong research to support the idea that your basic expenses decrease after retirement. Consumption tends to drop, either as a conscious decision or because of the fact that your lifestyle tends to take a different pattern than when you were working. For example, one study conducted in the U.S. found that there is a drop in grocery spending of about 7% and food expenditure overall at 8% to 9% in the first year of retirement.

"We have actually found that we spend less in retirement than we thought," said Vivien, a 58-year-old retired retail manager. "Since we are watching our money more closely than ever before, we have stopped spending on things that we really don't need. This doesn't mean that we don't enjoy ourselves, but my husband and I are amazed at the amount of money that we used to spend that we couldn't account for!"

In retirement, your expenditures for transportation, clothing, food and household goods tend to fall, while the money that you spend on leisure and health tends to rise.

There are some problems with the concept of the income replacement rate. Not everyone is the same and retirement spending is not a straight line throughout retirement. *Here are some variables to consider:*

• *Some Americans can retire on considerably less than they have been told they could.* However, others may not be able to retire on 200% or 300% of what they have been told, given the plans that they have. It will all depend on the life you want to lead, your health, the debt you are carrying or whether the house is paid for, etc.

• Spending patterns tend to change over time. For example, our experience is that most people tend to spend more in the first three years of retirement; this can be "emotional" spending to help adjust to a new reality, or it can simply be a newly retired couple repositioning their lives by buying the "toys" that they think they will need to get their retirement started!

• As you get older, your spending will likely turn more to family and health care. However, there will also be demands on your retirement finances that can cause substantial one-time spending. For example, buying a new car, helping a grown son with a business investment, lending your daughter and son-in-law money for a down payment on a new home or helping a grandchild pay for his or her education.

• An interesting American study in 2006 found that expenses actually do not change much if the level of income from work to retirement stays roughly the same.

## The "Three-Bucket Approach" To Retirement Spending

Do you have a "cash flow" personality or a "balance sheet personality"? While there is no right answer, there is a tendency in retirement to look at cash flow and financing month-to-month purchases. Regardless of their net worth, retirees tend to only look at the short term when it comes to the use of the financial resources they have.

As a result, retirees and their advisors consider available financial resources as one lump sum and don't break it down into the various components of retirement spending. For example, a client who has recently weathered a market downturn might complain to his advisor, "I have lost 25% of my retirement portfolio in the last year." In reply, the advisor asks the client, "Which part of your retirement portfolio is down?"

In this phase of life, it is more helpful for you to think about your retirement portfolio in terms of how you view your money psychologically. When you spend or save money in retirement, you are really drawing this money from three "buckets," or pools of capital. This allows you to consider both the short-term and long-term aspects of managing your money in retirement.

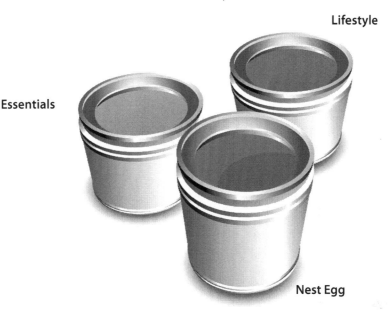

**Lifestyle**

**Essentials**

**Nest Egg**

### Essentials

This is the money that you spend on food, clothing, shelter and any other non-discretionary expenses. In other words, this is the amount of money you absolutely need each month to pay the basic living expenses one cannot do without. You might say you can't live without such things as cigarettes, holidays or new cars. This category only covers your basic human needs, as well as commitments such as insurance premiums and taxes that you are obligated to honour.

This money would normally come from a pension or fixed income. Since it covers your essential expenses, you don't want the money in this bucket to be subject to a lot of risk.

### Lifestyle / Enjoyment

This is the discretionary portion of the retirement pool. Money spent on anything that contributes directly to your enjoyment of life falls under this category. The key is to think about whether could do without any item in this category, if absolutely necessary.

Lifestyle is the toughest bucket to budget for if you are used to spending without any thought about where that money is going to come from. For example, a senior executive who is used to a substantial monthly paycheck continues to spend lavishly in retirement and then has to draw from savings in order to fund the same lifestyle. Many retirees fail to consider the idea of creating a retirement budget. However, the existence of such a budget is an important factor in creating a sense of "financial comfort." By "planning" your expenses and spending a small amount of time tracking them, you will continually reinforce your "piece of mind" and ongoing sense of comfort.

A challenge for retired boomers is to find ways to fund lifestyle without taking on additional debt, or considering their home equity as the salvation of their spending habits. As you think about your future, consider whether your lifestyle enjoyment expectations match the resources that you have allocated to the "fun" portion of your retirement.

You can take on more risk in your management of this money. Your withdrawals for lifestyle events, trips, dinners out, etc., will come from here, but you will need to have a pool of cash that feeds it and you will need some growth.

### Nest Egg

This is the pool of financial resources that allows you to "sleep at night." It includes home equity, your 401K and IRA, other assets that could be turned to cash, the long-term value of a pension plan and anticipated inheritances, as well as retirement savings and an investment portfolio. The concept of the nest egg is in part empirical and in part psychological. You really can't put a price on how much you will need in order to know that you will be "OK," and it will be different for everyone. *What do you need to have in reserve to ensure the following?*

- [ ] To not have to worry about outliving your money
- [ ] To pay for unexpected health care issues
- [ ] To not have to rely on friends and family for support
- [ ] To continue to enjoy the lifestyle that you want

If you need emergency money, you would have to draw it from this pool. Remember, though, that the more you take out of this pool or the more risk you expose it to, the more financial worries you will have.

At the end of your life, the money left over in the nest egg becomes your estate. During your lifetime, money required for emergencies or the unexpected will also be drawn from this reserve. As a result, you may be able to sleep soundly one week but may be thrown into insomnia the next if the nest egg takes an unexpected "hit" from unforeseen events.

## The Steps In Creating A Financial Plan

1. Agree on the goals and objectives for your overall retirement, including emotionally, financially, and contribution-wise.

2. Identify and agree on the - risks to the plan, including economic, market, and health risks.

3. Identify assets and income sources to support your retirement

4. Calculate your budget in first stage of retirement

5. Develop investment strategy to meet any additional income needs

6. Examine protection, legacy and estate planning goals

*Some other ways to create financial comfort in your planning*

- Understand your additional or potential sources of income.
- Consider all of your assets that could be turned into cash or provide income.
- Try to pay down all of your current debt, or at least consolidate it.
- In the first three years, keep close track of both your income and expenses.

What if there is a gap between what we want and what we have?
If you find in your Second Life that your resources don't meet your needs, what changes would you make?

☐    I would discuss my situation with my financial advisor.
☐    I would consider returning to work.
☐    I would make use of a line of credit or borrow.
☐    I would use the equity in my house to make up the shortfall.
☐    I would change my investment strategy to be more aggressive.
☐    I would change my lifestyle.
☐    I haven't thought about it.
☐    I would ignore it and hope for the best!

Are any of these really options for you or is there another way?

When you have assessed your current situation, you may find that there are gaps in meeting your goals, but there are always options for you to explore and things that you can do today to impact your future.

**1. Save more:** Take a closer look at your budget and leverage strategy, and make effective use of the cash flow you have

**2. Take less:** Many people overestimate retirement needs or need to find more realistic solutions. For example, should you take a big trip the year you retire rather than travel each year? do you really have to take out as much money as you are?

**3. Earn more:** Will you supplement your income in retirement through part-time work, will you retire in stages, etc.?

**4. Wait:** Maybe you don't have to retire and can continue to work and earn an income after traditional retirement.

**5. Spend Less:** Examine your lifestyle critically. Not everything has to be expensive. Eat at home, walk on the beach or in the park, or golf at home rather than on an expensive vacation.

## What Will You Do With This Information?

1. Work out a budget for your first year of retirement. There are many online budget tools (including the one mentioned above) that can help you forecast.

2. Consider how you would divide your spending into your Essential and Lifestyle buckets that we mentioned above. Then identify those funds (both present and future) that you have to fund your Nest Egg bucket. Note that this is not the same as a net-worth statement.

3. Clarify all sources of income that you have, including money from your investments, Social Security, pension income or other income, and then use your investment portfolio to make up the gap.

4. Can you earn more on your investments while still finding the correct balance?

5. Wait. What age is realistic to retire? Why 55? Remember you will live for 20 to 30 years, so when should your retirement start, or can you scale back rather than retire fully?

6. Even people who never want to officially retire need to have a fallback plan just in case declining health forces them to slow down.

7. Only you know how much income you will need to retire and what sacrifices, if any, you are willing to make to have a particular lifestyle. By taking control now, you significantly improve your chances of reaching your retirement goals.

## DID YOU KNOW?

• In a 2013 Ipsos Reid/Sun Life survey of pre-retirees, respondents expected 10% of retirement income to come from home equity, 30% from government plans, 27% from personal savings and 23% from employer plans, with the remainder coming from inheritances and other sources.

• In the same survey, when asked how satisfied they were with their retirement savings, 38% of respondents said overall they were satisfied.

• American men are more likely to be covered by a defined benefit pension plan or have IRAs or 401K plans than women.

# Sample Retirement Budget Sheet

| **Your Retirement Budget** | |
| --- | --- |
| Age | |
| Age today | |
| Age at retirement | |
| Years to retirement | |

| EXPENSES | TODAY | RETIREMENT |
| --- | --- | --- |
| HOUSING COSTS | | |
| Mortgage or rent | | |
| Property taxes | | |
| Maintenance/repairs | | |
| Home Insurance | | |
| Other | | |
| Total | | |
| **PERSONAL EXPENSE** | | |
| Grooming | | |
| Clothing | | |
| Holidays | | |
| Gifts | | |
| Auto Expenses | | |
| Auto Insurance | | |
| Gas/Maintenance | | |
| Other transportation | | |
| Total | | |
| **LIVING EXPENSE** | | |
| Groceries | | |
| Entertainment | | |
| Utilities | | |
| Telephone | | |
| Total | | |
| **MEDICAL EXPENSES** | | |
| Prescription Drugs | | |
| Medical Insurance | | |
| Total | | |
| OVERALL TOTAL | | |

| INCOME | TODAY | RETIREMENT |
|---|---|---|
| Work income | | |
| Other sources | | |
| Government pensions | | |
| Other plans | | |
| Total | | |

| SUMMARY | | |
|---|---|---|
| Income required | | |
| Estimated pension | | |
| Government benefits | | |
| Annual surplus/debit | | |
| Prescription drugs | | |
| Medical insurance | | |
| | | |
| Total | | |

# CHAPTER 28
## Managing Your Nest Egg In Your Second Life

### SOME THINGS TO CONSIDER:

• How does investment management change in retirement?

• How my approach to managing my investment portfolio change in retirement?

• What are the things I should watch for in my own behaviour around money?

• Should I consider different investment choices for retirement?

• Why is managing risk management so important?

• Am I an investor or a saver?

This chapter is not intended to be a complete discussion of investment management in retirement. That subject is beyond the scope of this book and is better dealt with in your conversations with a professional investment advisor. We want to bring up some issues that often affect retirees, particularly when it comes to their behaviour. We will address some errors in judgment in this chapter and better prepare you to speak to your advisor.

### Understanding Investment Risk In Retirement

"Risk" is the possibility that your plans may not go as expected. Over the life of your plan, there will be some risks that could affect whether you reach your goals or have to make your money work harder to keep up. Some of the most common risks that you will have to account for in your investment plan are:

**1** **Market volatility:** Someone once noted that "markets go up, then they go down, then they go back up again—that is just what they do."

Market volatility simply means that the value of your investments may not be at their optimum when you need to use the money.

What you can do about it: Remember that market volatility is a short-term phenomenon more than a long-term risk. In general, the longer your investment time horizon, the less volatile your investments will be. Two things that you can do to ease the impact of short-term markets on how your investments will reach your goals:

> • Don't try to outguess the market in the short-term and manage through markets, not to markets.
> • Hold on to your investments for longer periods of time or entrust your investments to managers who are not active market traders.
> • Diversity the mix in your investment portfolio with different types of stocks and fixed income investments (multiple asset classes)• If you have fixed income, try to vary your maturities so that something is always coming due. This takes some of the interest-rate risk away.

**2** **Political and economic risk:** So much of investment return is affected by investor sentiment. If people are optimistic, they are more likely to invest in the future; if they are pessimistic based on what they read in the morning newspaper, they will be less likely to commit.

What you can do about it: Since there will always be political and economic risks around the world that can affect your investments in the short run, change how you view the performance of your portfolio. Rather than compare your holdings to a benchmark like the S&P 500 or the Russell 2000, assess whether your investments are on track to reach the life goals that you set.

**3** **Investor risk:** If all investors were computers and could only react to the input they receive, markets would be much more predictable. Investor risk or behavior risk will not only come from how other investors are feeling in the short term and the impact of optimism or pessimism on short-term markets. It will also come from how you personally handle the day-to-day gyrations in your decision making.

What you can do about it: Don't allow yourself to be swayed by the media or investment gurus who say that they can predict where markets are going. Also, be aware of your own biases that influence your success as an investor. By working with an advisor who can help you keep your life goals in clear view, you can avoid being drawn into the whirlwind that today's investment markets often are. Remember, if it sounds too good to be true, it probably is!

There are certainly other risks to be aware of, including longevity risk or outliving your money, and inflation risk. A critical factor in managing all of these risks is in your behavior mentioned above. If you can become "unemotional" about the management of your nest egg, then effective risk management becomes just another part of the process.

Many retirees associate the term *risk* with their likelihood of losing their money. They will often look at the short-term moves in the market and the volatility of their investments as a measure of risk. Remember, however, that the longer you hold an investment, the less volatility you will see in its price. If volatility is a measure of risk for you, then holding an investment longer should take much of the risk away.

*There are several tools available to you to manage investment risk in retirement:*

**Insurance-based investments:** These are often called segregated funds or variable annuities, and can provide downside protection through the use of insurance while still providing some upside potential. As with any insurance solution, you are transferring a risk to an insurance company for a premium or payment. The insurance company in turn may provide you with a guaranteed income stream or payment. The guarantees associated with insurance-based solutions may help any number of the risks mentioned above.

**Asset allocation:** The old saying "don't put all of your eggs in one basket " is particularly applicable in retirement. By diversifying in different asset

classes (growth stocks, value stocks, domestic stocks, international stocks, short term bonds, government bonds, cash etc.) you can soften the effects of a falling stock market for example by holding other investments that might not be affected as much.

**Income-oriented investments**:   A wide variety of investment options may pay higher dividends or interest payments to help support income needs. These include options such as dividend paying stocks like utility companies, real estate investment trusts (REITs), municipal bonds, and structured notes. While all of these options can enhance your income stream, they each come with their own particulars regarding risk, tax treatment and liquidity. A seasoned financial advisor should be able to help you understand these options and if they fit your needs.

**Conservative or dividend-paying stocks:** While even the most conservative stock investments will still be affected by falling and rising markets, they may not experience the same kind of downside risk that other kinds of equities may experience. Many good quality companies pay dividends to shareholders and are often used as income vehicles. In addition, American tax laws treat dividend income in a different manner than interest or pension income through the Dividend Tax Credit.

**Mutual funds and managed portfolios:** These investments provide you with the benefit of diversification and professional management. While there is no guarantee that you will not be affected by market reversals, the presence of professional management and some level of automatic diversification can mitigate some of your risk.  As with any investment option, mutual funds and managed accounts should be monitored on an ongoing basis for their cost structure. can mitigate some of your risk. Watch for higher expenses in the funds you own (management expense ratios).

## The Role That Growth Plays In Your Portfolio
You may have been told that you should become very conservative in retirement and not expose your portfolio to unnecessary risk. The counter argument would be that you always want to make sure that your money is working for you. While being a   conservative investor almost always guarantees that you will get your money back, you may also lose money on it every year due to inflation.

The amount of growth that you need depends on whether there is a gap between what you will need versus what you have. There have been cases where a retiree has been too exposed to growth when it was unnecessary.

One example is a San Francisco dentist who brought his $4-million portfolio to an advisor in 2007 with the concern that it was not making as great a return as he would like.

The advisor, following instructions from his client, proceeded to expose the portfolio to more growth by increasing the allocation to the US and international stock markets.. The global economic meltdown occurred and the retiree went from having more than enough money to retire in the way he wanted to having to go back to work.

But don't let these horror stories dissuade you from including growth in your portfolio. If you take the "three-bucket approach" that we looked at in Chapter 27, it would make sense to expose a portion of your portfolio to the equity market. Discuss this with your advisor and reflect upon your ability to tolerate short-term risk. In fact, discussing the overall risk of your portfolio should be part of any annual or semi-annual "checkup" your advisor provides you.

## The Most Common Mistakes That Investors Make In Retirement

Despite our best intentions, we often make decisions that can't be considered rational. This has as much to do with the role that emotion plays in decision-making than simply making an error in judgment.

### 1. Taking a short-term view rather than focusing on the long term

When your financial advisor develops a plan for you, he or she has normally considered the risks that can be inherent in the market. It is virtually impossible to predict where markets will go, and investors often try to outguess the market in the short term.

Your investment plan is tied to your changing needs over time, rather than to where the markets are (if it isn't, then you should consider whether you are in the proper investment plan). If you change your strategies to focus on short-term market moves, you could potentially undo the overall plan.

### 2. Confusing 'saving' with 'investing'

The two are not the same. If you are a saver, you are not prepared to take on the risks that are normally associated with market investing; the trade-off, of course, is that your rate of return will not normally be enough to let you stay ahead of inflation.

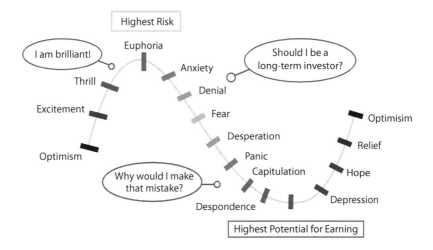

Investors seek higher returns and are prepared to take on some risk in order to generate higher returns. For most people, it is important to keep money growing and to maximize its ability to work without risking their nest eggs.

### 3. Trying to do it yourself

It may sound attractive to spend all day at your computer trying to figure out where markets are going and which stocks you should buy. After all, you are smart, like the markets and have enough time on your hands to really devote your brainpower to "beating the market." How hard can it be?

However, remember that if you are managing your entire retirement nest egg in this manner, you are at a considerable disadvantage. Professional managers have access to the latest information and still find it difficult to consistently outperform markets. This is not to say that you may not have success in the short run. However, individual investors will often make short-term decisions based on limited or poor information or emotion, and lose valuable pieces of their retirement nest egg.

The vast majority of individuals, partners or couples benefit from having a professional help watch over their nest eggs. Even if you enjoy trading at home, a "second opinion" is invaluable in your Second Life.

### 4. Not paying attention to transaction costs or fees

While there are some low-cost trading companies or online providers that you can work with, there may still be fees associated with your investments that will harm your overall return. Many mutual funds charge high fees that have to be paid whether the fund is up or down; some segregated funds will charge large fees for the insurance component of the investment. Again, this will affect the overall performance of your investments.

### 5. Trying to control what you can't control

Often, investors are caught up in their emotions and stop using common sense. There are things you can control and things you cannot. In retirement, you should try not to worry about things you can't really do anything about.

**What you can't control is:**

- Consistently picking winning stocks
- Consistently icking superior managers
- Timing the markets
- What the financial press says

**What you can control is:**

- Managing expenses — not paying too much in fees and charges on your investment portfolio
- Diversifying your portfolio — ensuring that the risk ensuring that the risk of your portfolio is within your "comfort zone" while utlizing multiple asset classes
- Minimizing the taxes you pay — paying attention to the tax consequences of the investments you make and ensuring that your portfolios are managed for tax efficiency
- Managing your mindset — your portfolio is focused on your life goals, not where the market is

## How Do We Tend To Make Investment Decisions In Retirement?

In the study of behavioural finance, much has been written about how investment decisions are actually made. *Here are some of the most common drivers of investment decisions in retirement:*

**Social Evidence:** Other people's behaviour matters: people do many things by observing and copying others; people are encouraged to continue to do things when they feel other people approve of their behaviour.

**Continuity Theory:** Habits are important: people do many things without consciously thinking about them. These habits are hard to change—even though people might want to change their behaviour, it is not easy for them to do so.

**The Principle of 'Reason':** People are motivated to "do the right thing": there are cases where money demotivates because it undermines people's intrinsic motivation; for example, you would quickly stop inviting friends to dinner if they insisted on paying you.

**The Impact of Your Values:** People's self-expectations influence how they behave. They want their actions to be in line with their values and their commitments.

**Fear of Loss:** People are loss-averse and hang on to what they consider 'theirs'. People are bad at computation when making decisions: they put undue weight on recent events and too little on far-off ones; they cannot calculate probabilities well and worry too much about unlikely events; and they are strongly influenced by how the problem/information is presented to them.

**Self-actualization:** People need to feel involved and effective to make a change; just giving them the incentives and the information is not necessarily enough.

As you approach or continue through your Second Life, you want to put yourself in right frame of mind and consider ALL of the various aspects of a retirement transition. This also requires a different skill set in an advisor. Many advisors are experts at accumulation and growth. Helping clients navigate a retirement transition requires a different skill set in an advisor. This disconnect or mismatching of the necessary retirement transition skills is one that is, unfortunately, very common.

## Working With Your Financial Advisor

There are many financial planning issues that may arise during retirement. Often, the advice of a good financial planner can save you both time and money, and give you peace of mind.

While there is a broad range of advisors to choose from, it is important for you to work with an individual who is not only knowledgeable but fits your personality and temperament. If you have a spouse or a partner, it is equally important that he or she feels comfortable working with the advisor you have chosen.

## What Do Advisors Do?

A professional financial advisor has the training to help you understand the key issues that you should plan for. during your transition and throughout your Second Life. . Through a variety of government agencies such as the Securities and Exchange commission as well as self-regulatory organizations such as FINRA, professional advisors have a strict code of conduct they must follow.

The main job of a financial advisor is to understand your life needs, concerns, opportunities and goals, and to match them with the financial resources that are available.

In many instances, this is a process of "bridging the gap" between what you want to accomplish in your retirement and what money is available to "make it happen."

## What A Professional Advisor Gets Paid For

It is easy an easy trap to mentally tie the fees you pay your advisor to the performance of an index or the overall markets. However, if you take the structured investing approach, then you are using your investment portfolio to achieve your life goals, not match or exceed the performance of an index.

A professional advisor who takes the structured investing approach is a different kind of advisor. This professional considers your life issues first and then works with you as a coach, guide, mentor and educator to help you keep your plans in focus. *There are three things that these advisors do to justify the fees they earn:*

**1** They provide you with clarity, helping you understand the things you should plan for, the things you should be worried about and the things that you shouldn't be worried about.

**2** They provide you with insight. Generally, these advisors have access to a lot of support in the advice they provide you, and often have decades of experience that gives them perspective. More important, however, is the insight they have into the clients they work with. Professional advisors take a structured and disciplined approach to understanding their clients.

**3** They work as your partner. These advisors provide you with counsel on an ongoing basis and are a valuable resource as you make the best use of your financial resources to reach your life goals.

Measure the success of your professional advisor in how you are doing in reaching your life goals. The approach the advisor has taken in managing your nest egg should be aligned with those goals. In short, he or she should be more concerned with where you are in respect to your life goals, rather than where the markets are at any given time.

*Here are the main financial issues that your advisor can help you with in your retirement planning:*

1. Working with you to clarify a reasonable retirement lifestyle plan that meets your needs and then developing the financial strategies to help you get there.

2. Helping you build an income strategy that will include your company pension, available government benefits, and additional income drawn from personal savings, etc.

3. Identifying potential tax issues that may affect you and ensuring that your income comes to you in the most effective way possible.

4. Developing an ongoing savings and investment strategy to keep your money working throughout your retirement.

5. Creating an estate plan with you so that your assets can be passed on to your loved ones or the recipients you choose in an efficient manner.

Remember that your advisor is at times an educator, a coach, a mentor

# CHAPTER 29
## *Creating an Estate Plan*

and a catalyst to help you do the right things to make your retirement as "worry-free" as possible.

### SOME THINGS TO CONSIDER:
• What issues will arise for your family and loved ones when you die?
• Have you considered how you would like to distribute the assets that you have accumulated over your life?
• Have you received professional advice to help you address all possible emotional, legal, tax and financial issues?

This chapter is not designed to be a definitive review of estate planning for two reasons. First, we want to cover some of the emotional issues that we see most often at a high level in order to give you some things to think about. Second, we believe that you and your loved ones are best served if you get professional advice.

### Why Do You Need An Estate Plan?

1. You can make sure that your family and others you care about are looked after when you can no longer make decisions.

2. You can maximize the amount available to your beneficiaries through effective tax planning  and minimize any shrinkage through effective estate tax planning.

3. You retain control over how your estate is managed and distributed.

4. If you have a business, you can influence how it is disposed of or who to pass it on to, and possibly avoid all of your hard work being undone.

5. The state won't gain control over how your assets are disposed of or who might benefit when you are gone.

## The Most Common Estate Planning Mistakes

### 1. Not having an up-to-date will and final instructions
While this is self-evident, it is always amazing to learn how many Americans either do not have an up-to-date will, or have no will at all! Not only can this cause a problem for your family and those close to you, but you also risk losing control over how your estate is distributed.

### 2. Not considering the emotional issues when you write your will
It is always hard to consider a world that doesn't include you, which may explain why many people don't have up-to-date wills. There may be emotional issues that you must consider as you draw up your will, including:

  • Blended families, and children from different marriages

  • Providing for a surviving spouse or partner, and ensuring that his or her standing will not be challenged when you are gone

  • Dealing with spendthrift children or children with substance abuse problems, and ensuring that they are protected from themselves

  • Creating an enduring power of attorney so that someone can act on your behalf if you cannot

### 3. Not having an executor who is aware of your requests and can ensure that your wishes are carried out.
Often, people don't pay enough attention to who they name as executor and what information that person needs to carry out his responsibilities and your wishes when the time comes. Do you have an executor that you have confidence in? Are you prepared to make a change if you are no longer comfortable with him? Does the executor have the confidence of members of your family or those who want to be looked after fairly?

### 4. Not considering all the assets that should be mentioned in your will (for example, collectibles, jewellery, real estate, art work, etc.)
Over the course of your life, you have accumulated many things that have either personal or financial value that go beyond your investment portfolio, real estate or bank accounts. How would you like to distribute these and who might be upset later? Are there family heirlooms or items

of emotional value to someone you care about that you should include in your will?

**5.**Not keeping your Beneficiary Designations current on your IRAs, Company Retirement Plans, and Insurance Policies.
We typically retire with numerous IRAs, 401(k)s or other company retirement accounts, and life insurance policies. Beneficiary designations dictate how those accounts will be transferred at your death, NOT your Will. The Beneficiary Form is "the law of the land" and overrides any directive in your Will or Trust. Keeping your Primary and Contingent Beneficiaries current to reflect your wishes is critical

### 6. Not having an Advanced Health Directive or Living Will in place
If you are concerned that your end-of-life wishes may not be carried out, you can create an Advanced Medical Directive or Healthcare Power of Attorney to ensure that your end-of-life medical care is what you want. This will take away any uncertainty your family may have if you can no longer speak for yourself.

**7.**Not establishing a Revocable Living Trust when appropriate – Certain individuals are couples may need to consider working with an attorney to draft a Revocable Living Trust or RLT. RLTs allow the individual to retain control of their assets while providing a greater level of control and distribution at death than a Will allows for. Another major mistake occurs when individuals create a trust but do not retitle their assets into the name of their trust. The result is like it never existed in the first place!

Remember, the clearer you are in these documents, the easier it will be for your loved ones later, and the more likely it will be that your assets will be distributed in the way that you wish.
Your estate-planning checklist

*Do you know where the following documents are?*

- ☐ Your will
- ☐ Your Living Will or Advanced Health Directive
- ☐ Your life insurance documents
- ☐ Important papers such as mortgage information, bank documents, etc.
- ☐ Your investment records
- ☐ The beneficiaries of your life insurance or IRAs

☐     The location of all of your assets

☐     The names of all of your advisors

## What Will You Do With This Information?

• Have you made a will?

• How many years has it been since you updated it?

• Have you made arrangements for a time when you may not be capable of making your own decisions? For example, have you assigned an enduring power of attorney?

• Have you thought about and/or prepared an advance medical directive in consultation with your medical practitioner and attorney?

• Do you know the location of all the documents listed in the documents checklist, and have you informed someone else of their whereabouts?

• Have you discussed with your attorney or advisor if a Revocable Living Trust or any other type of trust planning is appropriate for you? If so, when

was the last time your reviewed the provisions of the trust?

## DID YOU KNOW?

• Half of Americans do not have an up-to-date will or estate plan, according to Forbes.

• A will is a document that outlines how you would like to dispose of your assets.

• Your will should be reviewed whenever your circumstances change.

• Creating a Durable Power of Attorney allows you to decide who

# PART 8

*Your Second Life Plan*

# CHAPTER 30
## Creating a Financial Plan for the Future

will make decisions for you if you are unable to do so for yourself.

After reading this book and doing some of the thought-provoking exercises we have provided for you, it is now time to put together your retirement transition plan. *In this last chapter, we want you to organize your information so that you can lay out a plan--a plan for your Second Life.*

### What Does A Retirement Plan Mean?

A retirement plan doesn't have to be a 200-page book; you'll end up creating more stress if your plan is so complex that you can't internalize it. Our advice is to keep it simple.

Your retirement plan is a living document, which is to say that it should constantly reflect where you are in your life. As you think about your plan today, you are creating the foundation for your retirement. In fact, we have provided you with an extensive template to help you think about the issues that you should plan for in the future.

Sadly, most retirement plans are limited to financial plans. We strongly recommend having a financial plan and we believe that working with a professional financial advisor will provide you with relevant advice to help you build your investments. However, there is a "front end" to your

Your life needs, concerns, opportunities, purpose and goals

→

Your financial plan to achieve them

retirement plan that has to be in place FIRST before you commit to a financial plan.

Remember, your finances are the means to living your Second Life filled with purpose. Your finances are not your Second Life.

This book is designed to provide you with an understanding of your life issues and to help you clarify your vision. Then, you can take what you have discovered and formulate the financial strategy required to accomplish it.

## Your Planning Checklist Prior To Retirement

Readers of this book are not necessarily all on the verge of retirement. Some of you have 10 or more years to go and are trying to get a head start. Others have already retired and are going back to retool their plans, get back on track or confirm that they are already doing the right things.

*Here are some things that you can do in your run-up to retirement.*

**If you have more than 10 years to go:**

1. Read this book.

2. Create some basic life plans to guide your financial plan. It is not too early to think about where you might live, how long you want to work, some bucket list items (you don't have to wait for retirement to start these).

3. Develop your financial plans to ensure that you have an investment, income and savings strategy in place.

4. Start thinking about work/life balance. You are likely entering your peak earning years and the tendency is often to sacrifice lifestyle for work advancement (especially if you are male).

5. Review your insurance coverage to make sure that you have done enough to protect your family's lifestyle and income.

6. Create an estate plan, and ensure that your will, directives and trust documents are up to date.

7. Make sure that regular health checkups and a healthy lifestyle are now part of your life.

**Five to 10 years to go:**
1. Read this book!

2. If you haven't put any of the above things in place, do so now.

3. Revise your plans based on how close you are to retirement.

4. Make sure you would be financially OK in the event of involuntary retirement.

5. If you are planning to move or downsize, research possible locales, prices, amenities, etc. You want to have a fair idea of what you are facing.

6. Agree with the general timing of your retirement with your spouse or partner.

7. Start to think about retirement activities that you want to engage in and start incorporating them into your life now.

8. Have a clear view of the financial resources that you may have as you start your Second Life.

### Five years to one year:

1. Do the same planning activities as above, but review where you are now and take stock in your savings, investments, and income sources in retirement.

2. Discuss your plans with your current employer.

3. Reconsider the timing of your retirement if you need to, including working past your official retirement date.

4. Think about work opportunities, new hobbies or new careers. Start today to incorporate some of these into your life.

5. Think about your plans to replace or repair capital items such as your car, home, vacation home, etc.

### Within one year:

1. Look at all of the above plans and review your situation based on your previous goals.

2. Have a thorough health checkup and ensure that your health coverage is up to date and sufficient.

3. You may be eligible for Social Security. Check out what your options are at a local SSA office.

## Planning In Each Life Area

As you make your plans, remember to use the format that we provided you with in this book. It is a good template to keep you organized and ensure that you have covered all of the issues. Again, your purpose in retirement is driven by your values and what "work" you will engage in during retirement. Your health, your friends and family, and your "fun" time will all impact your Second Life in one way or another. And finally, your finances and financial comfort will help make it all happen.

## Reviewing Your Plan Regularly

For both your life plan and your financial plan, regular reviews are important. We recommend once a year for your life plan up to five years in advance and then every six months until you are one year away from retirement. Your financial plan should be reviewed with your advisor at least twice a year.

Questions to ask a "Second Life" Advisor
• What kind of experience or expertise do you have in helping people navigate through a retirement transition and then on through retirement?
• Have you taken any special trainging or received certifications in this area?
• What process do you use to develop a Second Life plan for your clients?
• How often are the plans reviewed? How often do you meet with your clie
• How do you stay current on investment strategies and solutions that focus on retirement income?
• Who do you turn to when we have healthcare, legal, tax or investment questions that we need answered for our plan?
• How do we compensate your for your advice and assistance with our plan?

## Work Sheets:

### My Plans For This Next Phase Of Life

| In this area of my life | I need to | This is what I am going to do |
|---|---|---|
| *My* Work | | |
| *My* Health | | |
| *My* Family | | |
| *My* Home | | |
| *My* Community | | |
| *My* Leisure | | |
| *My* Mind | | |
| *My* Spirit | | |

| Life-Planning Consideration | Some Financial Implications | Things to ask Financial Advisor about |
|---|---|---|
| *My* Work | • *Income Replacement*<br>• *Severance*<br>• *Bonus*<br>• *Phased-in Retirement*<br>• *Self-employment Possibility* | |
| *My* Health | • *Long-term Care*<br>• *Critical Illness*<br>• *Income Replacement*<br>• *Benefit Programs* | |
| *My* Money | • *Adequate Income*<br>• *Return vs. Risk*<br>• *Tax Implications*<br>• *Pension Plan Contributions*<br>• *Charitable Giving*<br>• *Healthy Savings* | |
| *My* Family | • *Income Protection*<br>• *Health Benefits*<br>• *Education Funding*<br>• *Critical Care for Parents*<br>• *Estate Planning* | |
| *My* Home | • *Mortgage Protection*<br>• *Financing Considerations*<br>• *Vacation Property*<br>• *Investment Property* | |
| *My* Community | • *Charitable Giving*<br>• *Team Sponsorship* | |
| *My* Leisure | • *Vacation Funding*<br>• *Hobby Costs*<br>• *Budgeting*<br>• *Income Replacement* | |
| *My* Mind | • *Financial Education*<br>• *Goal-setting for the Future*<br>• *Financial Comfort* | |
| *My* Spirit | • *Legacy Planning*<br>• *Charitable Giving or Tithing*<br>• *Estate Planning*<br>• *Travel Budgeting* | |

Here are some specific areas of your retirement life that you may want to plan for, based on your thoughts about the exercises that you have just completed.

## Answers to TRUE or FALSE *(from Chapter 1)*

**1. False.** The Retirement Lifestyle Center's survey of retirement workshop attendees who were already retired found that "health" was ranked as the number one key to a successful retirement. This doesn't mean that having enough money isn't important. Defining what is "enough" money means having a clear understanding of the life that you want to lead and then assessing how much that is going to cost you.

**2. False.** Many Americans are forced into retirement either by their companies or economic circumstances long before they are ready to quit working. In addition, the concept of "early retirement" suggests that retirement is far better than working (even if it is not).

**3. True.** Though not for the reasons that you may think. While there may be many reasons for retirees to be glum about their current circumstances, the fact is that half of all American adults regardless of age report being lonely, sad and/or depressed.

**4. False.** Increasing numbers of companies are providing work for the over-60 cohort. One of the major issues in the workplace today is that companies are trying to retain older workers. There are many opportunities for older workers to contribute their knowledge and experience.

**5. False.** This number has been widely bandied about by financial advisors and the press as a rule of thumb. The fact is that some retirees may be able to retire on 75% of their last year's income if they already own their own homes, don't want to change their lifestyle or intend to stay at home more. So much depends on the overall assets that an individual possesses rather than just their income level.

**6. False.** In fact, the longer you stay in the workplace, the greater your chances of living longer in the absence of other health problems, according to a study conducted by the National Academy on an Aging Society in Canada. Forty-eight per cent of workers over 65 reported that their health is "good to excellent" versus 26% of non-workers in the same age category.

**7. False.** Retirement isn't a life phase at all. Gerontologists have identified several distinct phases that American adults go through from ages 55 to 100-plus.

**8. True.** Work provides five basic needs. Retirees will find more success if they are able to identify what they gained from the workplace and then find a way to replace it.

**9. False.** In fact, retirement can be more stressful on relationships due to factors such as a lack of structure that result in stress, differences between the partners' ideas of retirement, hormonal differences that occur as we age, changing family and work dynamics, etc.

**10. False.** Most people feel that this statement may be true, but in fact the research doesn't support that conclusion. Both men and women can define themselves by their work, though men are more likely to do so than women. If you are define yourself by your work, you will find it hard to accept a new role in retirement without at least a small amount of adjustment!

**11. True.** Two out of three working Americans expect to run out of retirement savings by age 70 and four out of five anticipate running out before age 80, according to Mercer's latest Superannuation Index.

**12. True.** While mental inactivity is not the only cause of cognitive decline, it has now been shown to be one of the causes.

**13. False.** It depends on what kind of life you want and how you define "comfortable lifestyle." While having a million dollars in your retirement plan will certainly alleviate some of your financial worry, many people believe that they have to have a large lump sum in order to have any security or comfort in retirement. The fact is that there is no rule of thumb and the key is to assess the kind of lifestyle the resources that you have will purchase.

**14. True.** Stress-related diseases are the number one threat to healthy aging.

**15. False.** In fact, it is estimated that nine out of 10 American seniors will have at least one chronic condition after age 65 that will limit their mobility.

# FURTHER READING
## *How This Retirement Came To Be*

The word *retirement* took on much of its traditional meaning in the late 19th and early 20th centuries when our industrialized society moved from self-employment and "living off the land" to urbanization and working for employers.

Retirement provided less-than-satisfied workers with a hopeful vision of their golden years that would reward them for a lifetime of work. It was seen as a rite of passage, a sort of heaven on earth that workers could strive to achieve in their old age. The beginning of this "heaven on earth" was ingrained in our collective psyches to be age 65.

Like other industrialized countries around the world, retirement in Canada is an institutionalized concept. The first pension plan was introduced as early as 1889; men were eligible to receive their payments at age 65 and women at age 60. It is interesting to note that at the turn of the 20th century, the lifespan for American men was 55 and 59 for women!

Statistically, only half of the American population lived long enough to reach the qualifying age for Social Security, and those who made it that far could expect, on average, to reach 76 if they were male and 78 if they were female. To make matters worse, a tough means test meant that fewer than one in three actually received a pension.

Most countries have historically adopted age 65 as their formal retirement age. For example, the passage of Canada Social Security Act in 1935 set 65 as the earliest that Americans could collect their government pensions.

The idea of retirement as a permanent vacation gained prominence in the 1950s in the United States when insurance companies developed ad campaigns portraying retirees as happy people fishing, surfing, playing golf or sipping martinis—essentially enjoying the good life. In Canada, one major insurance company even came up with the concept of "Freedom 55"—setting age 55 as the benchmark for retirement bliss to begin.

*In the past century, the financial services industry and governments all reinforced a view that we retire because we:*

- Are old and can no longer contribute to the workplace
- Are taking jobs from someone younger
- Deserve to be rewarded for our loyalty and efforts

Over the years, insurance companies and the financial services industry have created a vision of retirement that made their products easier to sell. The vision of "having enough money to live your dreams" was the ultimate goal. Unfortunately, what we have today is an ingrained 50-year-old definition of retirement that is no longer a reality for most people.

Many of us accept retirement as a stage of life that automatically occurs in our latter years because that is the way society has traditionally looked at it.

We have been conditioned to expect it, long for it and plan for it. In fact, when someone mentions the word retirement, many of us have an image of what retirement is going to look like. For others, however, what retirement holds remains unclear.